Telling It Again and Again

REPETITION IN LITERATURE AND FILM

Telling It Again and Again

REPETITION IN

LITERATURE

AND FILM

Bruce F. Kawin *1945-*

Cornell University Press

ITHACA AND LONDON

First published 1972 by Cornell University Press.
Published in the United Kingdom by Cornell University Press Ltd., 2–4 Brook Street, London W1Y 1AA.

International Standard Book Number 0-8014-0698-6
Library of Congress Catalog Card Number 75-37753

PRINTED IN THE UNITED STATES OF AMERICA
BY VAIL-BALLOU PRESS, INC.

Librarians: Library of Congress cataloging information appears on the last page of the book.

For Marilyn

With thanks to Frank McConnell for his guidance and support, to Bert States for his careful reading of the manuscript, and to Murray Naditch, Champa Norzom, Sidhu, and Carol Sykes, for the hours of talking that got it off the ground.

Contents

Contents

One generation passeth away, and another generation cometh;
And the earth abideth for ever.
The sun also ariseth, and the sun goeth down,
And hasteth to his place where he ariseth.
The wind goeth toward the south,
And turneth about unto the north;
It turneth about continually in its circuit,
And the wind returneth again to its circuits.
All the rivers run into the sea,
Yet the sea is not full;
Unto the place whither the rivers go,
Thither they go again.
All things toil to weariness;
Man cannot utter it,
The eye is not satisfied with seeing,
Nor the ear filled with hearing.
That which hath been is that which shall be,
And that which hath been done is that which shall be done;
And there is nothing new under the sun.

—Ecclesiastes 1:4-9

And the light is sweet,
And a pleasant thing it is for the eyes to behold the sun.

—Ecclesiastes 11:7

Introduction

> Repetition, the re-experiencing of something
> identical, is clearly in itself a source of
> pleasure.
> —Sigmund Freud, *Beyond the Pleasure Principle*

Life takes its tone and character from repetition.
Ordinarily we consider those events that are capable of
being repeated, or those functions that insist on being
repeated, lower or more boring than those "once in a
lifetime," extraordinary, unrepeatable experiences that
we consider the true or interesting material of our life
histories. In conversation, we admire people who come
gracefully right to the point; the ultimate romantic experience of our culture is First Love, and its mature
replacement, the indissoluble open-breasted give and
take of marriage, is ordained unique, "till death do us
part." We "only live once"; we have to try everything
"once." Our belief is in history, the recording of
unique events occurring in linear time—time, that is,
which moves from time-point A to time-point A+1 to
time-point A+2 . . . without doubling back, and

which can conveniently be organized into past, present, and future. Events whose repetition is not extraordinary do not seem worth recording, in fact, hardly seem worth noticing. We rest secure in the uniqueness of our experience and identity.

What is true, however, is that many of the experiences we call extraordinary take on their personal importance either because they approximately repeat earlier experiences, or because they fulfill earlier expectations long rehearsed in fantasy; so that in both instances an event may have an air of familiarity about it even as it is occurring.[1] This is as true of a honeymoon as it is of a Proustian flash. It is further true that nothing actually felt, nothing real in its moment, is boring. Sexual intercourse, for example, loses neither its attractiveness nor its reality through being repeated; its felt intensity is entirely independent of previous experience. Why, since it is the same every time, does it not become boring? The answer is, because it is interesting to us: it proceeds from our basic needs, it is urgent and pleasant and present. It is outside time, and therefore outside futility.

Every day the sun comes up, stays up, goes down. We experience this cycle of light and warmth 26,000 times

---

[1] *Déjà vu* is of course the extreme case: we perceive something twice at once, and for the sake of mental coherence organize the perceptions into past and present. The basic defensive process of creating past-present-future time as a means of organizing experience that occurs in a continuous present should be noted at work here.

in an average lifetime, and find that not enough. What is more important for our purposes here: we do not find the cycle boring. It has rhythmic sympathy with the way we function. It is important. It is dependable. It is like us, and good and bad to us. It is not exhaustible; novelty is exhaustible. The search for novelty leads in the end to boredom. We are bored when we have run out of "interesting" things to do, or when our own lack of vital energy disgusts us. We are not bored with our personal obsessions, our natural functions, or the periodicity of nature—no matter how familiar to us they may be. The short-sightedness of the conventional view of repetition as repetitious is evident in the words of our most absurd contemporary politician, "You seen one redwood, you seen 'em all."

Are we bored with life because "it's been done already"? Do we wish our heartbeat would change color to keep us amused?

Our utilitarian attitude to time, that it ought not to be wasted, is ignorant of the nature of time. Time cannot be wasted any more than it can be invested; we do things not with it, but in it. The fact that something happens to us more than once cannot be used as moral criticism of the experience or of its "use" of time. What we principally need, in our relations with time, is the perceptual education that will allow us without anxiety (the urgency to *date*) to move as time moves, in the present—the only existing tense. Planning and regretting are metaphysically irrelevant. Our search for novelty proceeds directly from our anxiety about death, and from our misunderstanding of the nature of repetition. All experiences, like all propositions, "are of equal value." [2] On the night before the announced end of the world, those who have not understood all along the eternity of the present will run out and do something they have never done before, while the others will find an equal or greater sense of fulfillment by continuing to do what they have already found to be pleasant or necessary.

Repetitious is one thing, repetitive is another. It is to the colloquial interchangeability of the two words that most of the misunderstanding of the aesthetic and metaphysical concept of repetition is due. I will be using these words in the following senses:

Repetitious: when a word, percept, or experience is repeated with less impact at each recurrence; repeated to no particular end, out of a failure of invention or sloppiness of thought.
Repetitive: when a word, percept, or experience is repeated with equal or greater force at each occurrence.

Successful repetition depends both on the inherent interest of the recurring unit and on its context. Thus

[2] Ludwig Wittgenstein, *Tractatus Logico-Philosophicus,* trans. D. F. Pears and B. F. McGuinness (London: Routledge & Kegan Paul, 1961), 6.4.

we come to aesthetics. Some artists are better than others at interesting us in the things they think are worth repeating, or at giving their completed works such life that we will continue to re-experience them with pleasure. I do not enjoy Mozart's French Horn Concertos less at each hearing because I have heard them before; nor do I scold Lear that he has made his point, the last four *never*s are unnecessary. On the contrary: Lear's cries attain an intensity possible only in unremitting repetition; it is the power of his howl that is under discussion here, and its tendency, like Ginsberg's [3] after his, to open on areas of experience generally considered inaccessible to language.

This book treats repetition both as an aesthetic device in literature and film, and as a state of mind; for as I asserted at the outset, repetition is fundamental to human experience. It can lock us into the compulsive insatiability of neurosis, or free us into the spontaneity of the present tense; it can strengthen an impression, create a rhythm, flash us back, or start us over; it can take us out of time completely. My way of dealing with

[3] As Frank O'Hara reminds us in his poem, "Why I Am Not a Painter," what appears at the outset to be one's central subject may never appear in the finished work, but may nevertheless haunt and inform the work throughout. Allen Ginsberg has that kind of presence in this book. I am deeply indebted to him, and can at this point only refer the reader to the title poems of his books *Howl* and *Kaddish,* and in particular to "The Change" in *Planet News* (all available from City Lights Books, San Francisco).

all these functions is to concentrate on the demands
that varying conceptions of time can make on the progress of a work. Thus a good deal of space is given to
Marcel Proust, Gertrude Stein, Samuel Beckett, and
Alain Resnais.

In the first chapter, the neurotic, habituating, and
enervating properties of destructive repetition are considered. The second chapter covers what is conventionally considered the full range of the constructive powers
of repetition: from its ability to emphasize, interweave,
and lyricize to its utility in the creation of what E. K.
Brown calls "expanding symbols." [4] The third chapter
deals with works whose characters are in some way both
in and out of time, in particular Yeats's *Purgatory*. The
fourth chapter is concerned with the literature of the
continuous present, and the fifth deals directly with the
drive past language to silence. Implicit in this construction is my sense that there are two sorts of narrative
time: one that builds and one that continues. The first
is appropriate to emphasis, Tolstoyan interrelations,
and so forth, but is in conflict with the ongoing nature
of the line of words or strip of frames, which tend to
keep the audience in a continually new present tense
and to undermine the reliability of that audience's

[4] E. K. Brown's *Rhythm in the Novel* (Toronto: University of
Toronto Press and London: Oxford University Press, 1950) offers
an extremely interesting introduction to the aesthetics of "repetition with variation." It deals primarily with E. M. Forster's
A Passage to India.

memory. The aesthetics of this second narrative time depend on repetition, and point out the tendency in repetition itself to lead us not simply into the present, but into the timeless.

Despite this freedom of range, my discussion is limited in many ways, of which the most important follows. The aesthetics of repetition cannot really be separated from the aesthetics of change; nevertheless I have chosen to emphasize the former. I simply ask the reader to bear in mind that except in the context of some change or progression, any repetition taking place in advancing time is undiscussable. The growth of the work, even from one identical line to another, makes exact repetition impossible: and this, in a sense, is my point. This book is really about the aesthetics of near-repetition. Repetition is a nonverbal state; it cannot be committed to any art that occurs in time. Near-repetition—which, given the strictures of advancing time and linear syntax, is the most that can be done in words or notes or frames—succeeds by intimating, and to a greater or lesser degree almost by containing, the nature of this necessarily nonverbal state. The discussion of this state is reserved for the final chapter; until then, I refer to intense levels of near-repetition as if they were repetitions, since they are, in any case, all that art can do.

I will try to show how repetition, the key to our experience, may become the key to our expression of experience. "Man cannot utter it," [5] but he can utter around it. He can, through repetition, "make it manifest."

But because every great creative force can be destructive, we begin by exploring the distinction between "all things toil to weariness" and "the light is sweet."

[5] All Old Testament quotations are taken from *The Holy Scriptures* (Philadelphia: Jewish Publication Society, 1917). Metaphor, too, "utters around it"; but repetition has the unique ability to bring us within reach of the nonverbal, even to generate nonverbal states of apprehension.

1. Destructive Repetition

What can it possibly mean to be part of
something that's over?
—Lauren Bacall, quoted in *Life,* April 3, 1970

We enjoy choruses when they are sung and skip over
them when they are printed. Choruses do not present
new information, and the reading mind fills in the experience of a chorus as it jumps from verse to verse. We
would suspend our rush to novelty if the printed song
could move us in its own time, manifest the developing
unity that we do feel when it is sung. We are bored and
impatient when the new turns out to be old. What the
careful reader of this book will discover is that even a
repetition can be new. The question is, what literary
techniques are available to provide for naked words
that sense of direction and development, that faith in
the rightness of a repetition, which music performs in a
song? Unfortunately it is often easier to recognize a failure than a success. Let us consider a series of related problems, both aesthetic and psychological, having as their

common element repetition that either has gone flat or has actually had a destructive effect on its material.

"Joke Worn Thin by Repetition"

Allen Funt's film, *What Do You Say to a Naked Lady?* (1969), includes many hidden-camera confrontations between unclothed models and embarrassed, clothed passers-by. It was criticized by one reviewer for running out of ideas; evaluating the film as a joke rather than as a neosociological accumulation, this reviewer wrote: "By the last segment, the joke has worn thin by repetition. I mean, how many things CAN you say to a naked lady?" [1] Although he disliked the film for not having enough novelty, his review leads us to conclude that the film's real problem lay *in* its search for novelty. We infer that Funt's approach (or the prevailing critical attitude which led the reviewer to expect such an approach) was to think of as many possible *different* ways of exploiting what one might say to a naked lady, and to mix them in such a way that the audience would not become bored, would not, that is, become *aware* of what Funt might fear would be non-dynamic repetition. In such a case, it is not hard for the audience to recognize a fundamental lack of invention.

Out-and-out repetitions are an aesthetic challenge;

[1] Bernard Drew, "Joke Worn Thin by Repetition," Gannett News Service; in "Showtime," *Ithaca Journal,* May 9, 1970, p. 9.

masking them in novelty is often merely a dodge—artistically insincere, proceeding from a lack of faith in one's material or audience.

This point is best made by contrast with a sturdy joke, repeated with obvious relish—a passage no reader would be tempted to skim.

Mr. Podsnap's world was not a very large world, morally; no, nor even geographically: seeing that although his business was sustained upon commerce with other countries, he considered other countries, with that important reservation, a mistake, and of their manners and customs would conclusively observe, "Not English!" when, PRESTO! with a flourish of the arm, and a flush of the face, they were swept away. Elsewise, the world got up at eight, shaved close at a quarter-past, breakfasted at nine, went to the City at ten, came home at half-past five, and dined at seven. Mr. Podsnap's notions of the Arts in their integrity might have been stated thus. Literature; large print, respectfully descriptive of getting up at eight, shaving close at a quarter-past, breakfasting at nine, going to the City at ten, coming home at half-past five, and dining at seven. Painting and Sculpture; models and portraits representing Professors of getting up at eight, shaving close at a quarter-past, breakfasting at nine, going to the City at ten, coming home at half-past five, and dining at seven. Music; a respectable performance (without variations) on stringed and wind instruments, sedately expressive of getting up at eight, shaving close at a quarter-past, breakfasting at nine, going to the City at ten, coming home at half-past five, and dining at seven. Nothing else to be permitted to those same va-grants the Arts, on pain of excommunication. Nothing else to be—anywhere! [2]

It is clear that such an outright use of repetition can strengthen, while the chief effects of unsure repetition are loss of audience attention (boredom) and enervation of one's material.

Inappropriate Repetition

The Reverend Gail Hightower, in Faulkner's *Light in August,* is an extreme example of the rigidity char-acteristic of neurotic repetition. He is trapped in an instant of time that occurred before his birth—the shotgun death of his grandfather while stealing chickens in the Civil War. He attempts, in being called to Jeffer-son, to live through and nullify the shame of this mo-ment, but finds himself instead compulsively involved in it: reliving it in his sermons, abandoning the present, becoming his own and the dead moment's ghost. High-tower repeats the obsessive instant until he is the instant.

One of the principal characteristics of useless repeti-tion is that it locks a work or a life into an unfulfillable compulsive cycle. Hightower feels that his life "ceased

[2] Charles Dickens, "Podsnappery," *Our Mutual Friend.*

before it began";[3] he allows himself to become rigid, through an obsession with the past that he cannot transcend. This condition is true of many of Faulkner's characters—Sutpen and Rosa Coldfield, for example, repeatedly described as "rigid" and "indomitable." The activity produced by the obsession may be furious and even useful—the construction in *Absalom, Absalom!* of Sutpen's Hundred—but it cannot be said to represent progress for the person obsessed. As Lawrence Kubie remarked, "No compulsive work drive has ever healed itself through working, however successfully."[4]

It is a terrible thing to live someone else's life—to repeat, as Hightower does, a life other than one's own; but certainly that is a rare occurrence. Hightower's experience has relevance to the more common problem of inappropriate repetition. We are often forced to relive dead and rigid aspects of our *own* lives rather than live creatively, in freedom, in continuing time.

Kubie's *Neurotic Distortion of the Creative Process* argues that creativity consists in "the capacity to find new and unexpected connections"[5] and that it is the

[3] William Faulkner, *Light in August* (New York: Random House, 1932); reference is to the Modern Library hardcover edition, p. 418.

[4] Lawrence S. Kubie, *Neurotic Distortion of the Creative Process* (New York: Noonday, 1961), p. 142. See also his p. 64.

[5] Kubie, p. 141. Clearly Kubie's terminology is indebted to Freud's (discussed below).

preconscious—an area of the mind neither conscious nor unconscious that condenses, intuits, and contains information that is accessible on need—that is our true creative faculty. Both the conscious and unconscious have relatively rigid associative systems. The word "eraser," for example, is associated by the conscious with a rubber mark-remover; but it might be associated by the unconscious with some terrible childhood trauma and make a person inexplicably anxious. The preconscious, however, can make an imaginative leap from "eraser" to *Oedipus Rex* and produce the material for such a novel as Alain Robbe-Grillet's *The Erasers*— when its freedom is not compromised by the inaccessibility of the unconscious symbolic process. While conscious symbols may be so clear as to be mundane, unconscious symbols are "impenetrable and fixed disguises." This rigidity of association ultimately directs the associations made by the preconscious. Material is offered to the intuitive faculty with hidden and unmodifiable meanings. The unconscious forces our "unacceptable conflicts . . . aims, and impulses" out into the world, each time in its same disguise, into our dreams, our "slips," our behavior, and our art. Both the impulse and the disguise must repeat; they can be neither modified nor resolved by this process. This rigidity in repetition is the chief characteristic of neurotic activity: "Any moment of behavior is neurotic *if the processes that set it in motion predetermine its automatic repetition,* and this irrespective of

the situation or the social or personal values or consequences of the act." [6]

Until we resolve the conflicts that rigidify our associations, every attempt we make to create something new
(a *second* novel) will be twisted into a re-expression, in
however cleverly modified a form, of our concealed
concerns.[7]

The artist's usual defense against a psychological
reading of his works is that his art consists in the variations he performs on his one true subject in his carefully perfected, claimed, and deeded style; it is the art,
not the subject, that is important; don't mistake me for
my persona. Many artists assume that their most vital
material comes from the unconscious—that an unresolved conflict is the best insurance a creator has of not
"running dry." Can you imagine, they ask, a happy
Dostoevski? Kubie astutely points out that unless the
artist is healthy, unless he can make new associations as
they are appropriate to the work before him, he can
produce dreams but not art—very likely the same
dream each time. The fact that his style and his preoccupations spring from the same unresolved material,
and therefore appear well suited, may keep him from
realizing that both may be uncreative and compulsive.

[6] Kubie, p. 21.

[7] See also Raymond Durgnat, *Films and Feelings,* p. 27: "Always when we speak of an artist's 'personal style' we might as
well speak of his 'recurrent content.'" This applies to technique
as well as to subject matter.

Telling It Again and Again

We must ask whether, in his perfection of an "appropriate" or successful style, the artist is forging a tool to facilitate the exploration and mastery of his material or building a set of adjoining cages: one for the material, the other for himself.

Repetition Compulsion

In his essays *Beyond the Pleasure Principle* (1920) and *Recollection, Repetition, and Working Through* (1914), Sigmund Freud identifies the compulsion to repeat as a means of mastering difficult material, as an obstruction and aid in psychotherapy, and as the key to the death instinct. Its application to the problem of memory will concern us more when we come to Beckett and Proust. In the practice of psychotherapy, repetition is encountered as a hindrance to memory—or more properly, as a means of remembering that can be exploited in a transference situation. The analyst would like to be able to help his patient *remember* a trauma and see it in the perspective of the present; [8] but what usually occurs is that the patient acts out his trauma again in the present, without any critical distance—without even being aware that he is in fact repeating earlier behavior. The analyst exploits this repetition by

[8] Sigmund Freud, *Beyond the Pleasure Principle,* trans. James Strachey (New York: Liveright, 1924); references are to the Bantam paperback edition, pp. 39, 67.

creating in the transference a "playground" for the material, "replacing his whole ordinary neurosis by a 'transference-neurosis' of which he can be cured by the therapeutic work." [9] The patient repeats because his repressions keep him from remembering the traumatic material, and because the material is, even so, trying to express itself.

When the motivating energy of this urge to repeat originates in the unconscious, that impulse is called the "repetition compulsion." Freud sees this compulsion also in the functioning of the instincts, all of which attempt to relieve tension, returning us to that state of relaxation presumed to have existed before we became sexually excited, or hungry, or alive. The death instinct is an urge inherent in organic life to return to the inorganic, to repeat that earlier state.

On an instinctual level, the repetition compulsion puts us through tension-arousing and -dispelling cycles: making us live, letting us die. On a psychotherapeutic level, this compulsion acts in the service of the most immediate and inaccessible form of memory, forcing us not to remember but to relive unmastered material. We may also find ourselves repeating, rather than remembering, traumatic experiences outside the therapeu-

[9] Sigmund Freud, "Further Recommendations in the Technique of Psycho-Analysis: Recollection, Repetition, and Working Through," *Collected Papers*, trans. Joan Riviere (London: Hogarth Press, 1949), Vol. II, 374.

tic context: "Thus," as Freud observed, "we have come across people all of whose human relationships have the same outcome." [10] When every one of our love affairs ends badly, and for the same unstated reasons, no matter how different the lovers; when every business venture turns mysteriously against us; when we are driven to help others yet fated to see them reject us— then we may assume that we are in the grip not of an avenging God, but of our own compulsion to repeat.

Freud observed not only the automatic, destructive, and death-serving effects of repetition. He also saw that repetition can operate in the interests of the pleasure principle:

Nor can children have their *pleasurable* experiences repeated often enough, and they are inexorable in their insistence that the repetition shall be an identical one. This character trait disappears later on. If a joke is heard for a second time it produces almost no effect; a theatrical production never creates so great an impression the second time as the first; indeed, it is hardly possible to persuade an adult who has very much enjoyed reading a book to re-read it immediately. Novelty is always the condition of enjoyment. But children never tire of asking an adult to repeat a game that he has shown them or played with them, till he is too exhausted to go on. And if a child has been told a nice story, he will insist on hearing it over and over

[10] Sigmund Freud, *Beyond the Pleasure Principle*, pp. 44–45.

again rather than a new one; and he will remorselessly stipulate that the repetition shall be an identical one and will correct any alterations of which the narrator may be guilty. . . . Repetition, the re-experiencing of something identical, is clearly in itself a source of pleasure.[11]

What we shall be discussing as an aesthetic problem— the relative uses and merits of repetition and novelty— is here explained away as a function of psychic maturity. This passage does not take into account the pleasure felt by an adult at certain repetitions in nature and art and conversation—or if it does, it posits that none of us ever outgrows his infancy completely.

Habit

We are assaulted by stimuli from all sides; they have an intense reality which, if we were continually aware of it, would probably so overwhelm us as to make us unable to function. We have a skin which keeps our rawer tissues from too great an environmental onslaught; anyone with an open wound is aware of this suddenly. We have a skin on our senses too: we are not meant to receive all that is out there. We have blinders and repressions and clothes and preconceptions and houses and institutions and habits. According to Freud,

[11] *Ibid.,* p. 66.

"protection against stimuli is an almost more important function for the living organism than *reception of* stimuli." [12]

In a 1962 Pacifica Radio program and later in a Hubley Studio cartoon, Robert M. Hutchins described the life and philosophy of a near-fictional neo-Freudian, Zuckerkandl, whose view that the aim of life is death led him to such startling insights as the idea that the only reason we get out of our beds in the morning is that we cannot take them with us; we adapt to this reality by so anesthetizing our waking/walking experience that it is as if we had our beds with us all day. Freud said we should make our unconscious conscious; Zuckerkandl said we should make our conscious unconscious. He asks, which leg did we put into our pants first this morning? What was the train like today? Such experiences are usually lost to us by virtue of their having become habitual. Repetition without insight or excitement creates routine, takes the life out of living, and *cannot cause us pain.* The idea is to make our entire lives routine, so that we will not feel anything—to thicken the skin on our senses.

Such a system occupies the border between the dedicated routine of Mr. Podsnap and the existential-anesthetic routine of Beckett's Mr. Knott. Certainly when we come to habit, we have come to the most destructive

[12] *Ibid.,* p. 53.

effect of repetition, for it is the doing of things over and over, each time with less energy and less interest, that is the root of repetitiousness in literature—on the way to anesthesia: the cliché we do not even notice, the dead word, the dead work,[13] the zombie.

Proust's *A la Recherche du temps perdu* will occupy us throughout; I introduce it here because one of its great subjects is the oscillating ascendency in our lives between habit and suffering—between experience that is fenced in and neutralized and experience that is intense and perhaps painful. The flash of forgotten reality into a dead and comfortable world is an act of repetition—"the re-experiencing of something identical"— that undoes the routinizing repetitions of a life of habit. Beckett's master's thesis, *Proust,* tells us much about both authors.

"The pernicious devotion of habit," writes Beckett, "paralyses our attention, drugs those handmaidens of perception whose cooperation is not absolutely essential." Beckett's paraphrase of Proust prepares the experiential ground for *Watt,* where in Mr. Knott's household everything is governed by routine, the simple and

[13] I mean both work that has no internal energy and work that trains its audience not to respond. Before going on, I would like to call attention to Joe Brainard's masterful one-page story, "Alice": one of the greatest habit-as-repetition nightmares in American literature (Paris: *Art and Literature* 11 [1967]).

unknowable, and for *Endgame,* where at the end of the world Hamm asks continually whether *it is time yet* for his painkiller, the anesthetic within anesthetic. Habit protects us from awareness or sensation, anxiety or pain. Life is a succession of habits, between which "for a moment the boredom of living is replaced by the suffering of being." [14] Watt feels pain intensely, and is anxiously aware of the reality of Mr. Knott's household, only in those moments when he is given new duties (feeding the dog) or moved (in, upstairs, out), or when something unusual or inexplicable occurs (the visit of the piano tuners). He is "comforted" by explanations, logical correspondences; it is all right for things to occur, as long as they can be explained. But the household is intuitively posited; one cannot entirely describe its pots with the word "pot." As long as an object or situation remains imperfectly described and apprehended, it produces anxiety in Watt, whose language bounds into new languages in an attempt to describe consciously what is beyond the accurate reach of language: that which Wittgenstein realized must be passed over in silence.[15] Where the language is adequate, there is no disturbance.

[14] Beckett, *Proust and Three Dialogues* (London: John Calder, 1965), p. 20.

[15] Wittgenstein, *Tractatus,* 7. (His Sabbath, as G. C. Kinnear pointed out to me. The limits of his world are built in 1–6.)

Our habits insulate us from pain; they also, by keeping us from discovering life with a thinner skin, spare us the final pain of leaving pleasure by keeping us from realizing the potential intensity of that pleasure. It is safer not to feel, but rarely do Beckett or Proust allow their characters such banal security.

Hemingway

Like *Watt, The Sun Also Rises* is a constructively repetitive novel about destructive repetition. Jake Barnes's generation is "lost" to the extent that it moves on the surface of life, goes from café to café, drinks the same drinks or, like the couple in "Hills like White Elephants," tries new drinks—lives perpetually unfulfilled and uncreative in a paradigm of repetitive activity that accomplishes nothing: in a world where habit and novelty stagnate and merge.

The love-encounters of Jake and Brett, in their terrible frustration, determined continually to rebegin and never climax—like any neurotic drive—are their own specific hell:

"Oh, darling," Brett said, "I'm so miserable."
I had that feeling of going through something that has all happened before. "You were happy a minute ago."
The drummer shouted: "You can't two time—". . .

I had the feeling as in a nightmare of it all being something repeated, something I had been through and that now I must go through again.[16]

The scenes with Brett are intense in their repetition just as the scenes in the cafés are dissipating in theirs. The reason that the repetition in the former scenes is felt stronger each time and in the latter is felt less is that the love-meetings generate tension but do not release it, while the more pointless daily activity of the expatriates is antidramatic, sapping energy rather than building it to some romantic or creative catharsis. Even the "dramatic" fights and affairs are boring—novelty of which one tires.

Jake's full-blooded impotence cannot have its tension reduced; no routine can dispel his frustration. Thus he is our best observer of the role of destructive repetition in the lives of others—perhaps using repetition in his lean prose as a sort of revenge of the damned, using it stylistically to emphasize the persistence of life, the reality of reality, since for him there is no escape from "the suffering of being." Routine makes his conscious conscious.

It is generally true of Hemingway's love-writing that love that can be fulfilled will be frustrated, either be-

16 Ernest Hemingway, *The Sun Also Rises* (New York: Scribner's, 1926); reference is to the Scribner Library paperback edition, p. 64.

fore or after fulfillment. Jake Barnes is castrated from the beginning. The narrator of *A Farewell to Arms,* slow to open up to his woman, is indirectly guilty of her childbed death, and ends the novel alone and more wounded than he could ever have been had he not let down his emotional guard.[17]

Hemingway's tough style is the index of his withdrawal and fear, the hardness he throws onto experience. None of his major works is free from projections of phallic guilt—perhaps this accounts for his popularity in our industrial, nuclear age. Henry kills Catherine. The Old Man's fish is eaten. In *For Whom the Bell Tolls,* where Robert Jordan comes as close to fulfillment as any Hemingway character since Nick Adams (but see "The End of Something," "A Very Short Story," "Cross Country Snow"), after the tough capable hero has won the boyish unwinnable woman (formerly prostituted by superaggressive fascists), and after Hemingway has lost control of his style in lavish description of the transcendent event, and after the final dynamite orgasm has succeeded, the fellow is killed. It is like the Czech film *Closely Watched Trains* without a sense of humor. Jake Barnes is frustrated but safe. His feelings are free to pressure-cook forever, like those of the inhibited romantic (Werther, Yeats).

The problem of killing our feelings before they

---

[17] But the prose stays tough—a final defense, and an indication that Henry is covering his wounds as he narrates the story.

threaten us is general. Few writers since Whitman have been able to consider how great are the tensions and implications of a touch; even for the narrator of *Song of Myself* it is "too much." And just as repetitions, in the construction and reinforcement of routine, dull our awareness and keep us from pain in our daily lives, they can keep us from experiencing with the intensity that is there already, in the instant and in ourselves, our moments of love. Hemingway uses repetition constructively, in style and plot, to reinforce the solidity of his objects, emotions—such as they emerge—and preoccupations; he castrates his characters not with repetition but with some personal plot-linked idiosyncrasy. The state his characters are in after he has castrated them, however, is analogous to the state brought about in the emotional memory by a process of destructive repetition that I choose to call "falsification of reality." The end— an inability to feel completely without some neutralization either of the object or of the subject—is similar.

The Falsification of Reality

Freud pointed out that by repeating an experience we may become master of it; he described a child's game of throwing away certain favorite toys again and again, an activity through which the child overcame his own fears of rejection.[18] Repetition in this case is op-

[18] Freud, *Beyond the Pleasure Principle*, pp. 32–36.

erating to remove the emotional content from a mental experience. As I shall attempt to show later, beginning an experience or its description over and over can have the effect of discovering or strengthening the reality of that experience; but in the human memory, repetition more often than not is the destroyer and not the saver: a neutralizer, habituator, and falsifier.

According to Proust we have two sorts of memory. When we try actively to remember something, that is voluntary memory; and when something comes into our head without our prompting, that is involuntary memory. When Marcel tastes the madeleine and remembers Combray, that is involuntary memory. When he tries to recreate an experience of involuntary memory he has just had—stepping on an uneven cobblestone and flashing to Venice—and is unable to, and feels the reality of that involuntarily summoned past fading, that is the action and destructiveness of voluntary memory.

Beckett interpreted the fading of the involuntarily remembered reality not so much as the action of voluntary memory as that of habit: the system of repressions that keeps us from the pain of experience. Leaning to unbutton his boot, Marcel remembers his grandmother, realizes in pain who she was and that she is dead:

But already will, the will to live, the will not to suffer, Habit, having recovered from its momentary paralysis, has laid the foundations of its evil and necessary structure, and the vision of his grandmother begins to fade and to lose that miraculous relief and clarity that no effort of deliberate remoration can impart or restore.[19]

Voluntary memory protects us from intensity, whether the intense instant is one of remembering or of living; this is in effect an instance of memory protecting us from itself. "Efforts at deliberate remoration" constitute voluntary "repetitions," which cannot create the true, involuntarily triggered subjective repetition. Whether this is the effect of habit or of more neurotic systems of repression, the reality of the vision is equally lost.

We may bring voluntary memory into play on purpose to remove the threatening component of an experience. We may remember something frightening so many times that it will no longer be frightening, just as the child's game gave him mastery over his fears of rejection. Often, however, this is a game not of mastery but of submission.

There are some things that the more we try to remember, the more we are unable to—and the more we succeed in remembering, the more we drain. A vision such as Marcel's of his grandmother may come involuntarily, but it is possible, by trying immediately after such a flash to capture "that miraculous relief and clarity" voluntarily, to set seal after seal on the experience—

[19] Beckett, *Proust,* p. 43.

to flatten it, in fact to kill it. Attempting to repeat an experience in memory makes accurate re-experience impossible. We have to remember something less than real; to remember without "the suffering of being," we have to falsify. Once this intense reality has been taken out of the memory, however, we feel the natural urge to know what it is we have forgotten; the more secretly assured we are that felt repetition has been blocked, the more ardent our efforts at re-evocation become.

Writing about something real, or something that is real in one's imagination, is similar to repeatedly remembering anything. For an artist to describe a scene in his head, the scene must be called up many times until the proper words for it are found. By that time the artist is lucky if he can at all remember the scene as he first conceived it. What is more likely is that what he has substituted for its reality on paper has also taken the place of the original fantasy in his head. The effect is just as completely the fictionalization of reality when he turns a mental reality—the fantasy, the story, the past, the idea of the emotion—into a delimited captured structure on paper as when he performs the same examining and describing and rearranging disservice in memory. We take our pasts and what we do to them is exactly analogous to the half-accurate art of autobiography.

Formulated, the experience has the reality of a formulation. Spinoza, *Ethics*, V: "An emotion ceases to be an emotion the moment we form a clear idea of it." It is art now, or adapted memory—a process of substitution that is the basis of much art; and the better the substitution, the better the art—the worse the chances of the accurate survival of the experience. Genet: "The work flames and its model dies." [20]

Say one word to yourself thirty times—"meaning," for example, or your name.[21] It loses its definition, becomes abstract and absurd. It also becomes a religious tool: once it has lost its literal associations, it addresses the silence. Now remember one memory many times.

We are in a psychic variant of the Principle of Indeterminacy, of which a concise description follows:

This principle, which was formulated by Werner Heisenberg (in 1927), and which plays a fundamental role in quantum mechanics . . . states that it is impossible to specify or determine simultaneously both the position and velocity of a particle as accurately as is wished. It is, to be sure, possible to fix either of these quantities as precisely as desired, but only at a price, for the greater the precision in one, the greater the inevitable lack of definiteness in the other.[22]

[20] Jean Genet, *Miracle of the Rose*, trans. Bernard Frechtman (New York: Grove Press, Black Cat, 1967), p. 244.

[21] After finishing this book I ran across Diane Wakoski's brilliant poem, "Filling the Boxes of Joseph Cornell" (*Inside the Blood Factory*, New York: Doubleday & Co., 1968), which says all of this beautifully.

[22] *Encyclopaedia Britannica* (1953), XXII, 679: "Uncertainty Principle."

To extrapolate metaphorically: it is possible to remember either the physical component of an experience, or the mental, but not both. In a Hemingway
world, one can successfully do *or* vulnerably feel. The
falsification of reality in art or memory comes about
from the *attempt* at repetition, the action of voluntarily remembering; by trying to "perceive" the event
again, we change it. Similarly, in photographing sub-
atomic particles, it is necessary either to bombard those
particles with other particles or to deprive them of some
of their energy, so that the measuring inevitably changes
the object measured, besides making perfectly accurate
measurement impossible:

It is to be emphasized that in making observations on a
system, it is necessary to exchange energy and momentum
with it. This exchange of necessity spoils the original properties of the system. The resulting lack of precision with
which these properties can be measured is the crux of the
uncertainty principle. In the microscope example, for instance, the momentum of the particle was rendered uncer-
tain by the impact with the light quantum by which it was
being observed.[23]

Proust almost offers us a way out of this dilemma
through the invocation of involuntary memory: we *can*
re-experience an event—recapture the past—when that
event simply pops up in front of us as something we had

[23] *Ibid.*, p. 680.

"forgotten" and which had accidentally been associatively evoked. But to go after it and try to hold on—position *and* velocity—is like holding the hand of someone who has just died. In *A Farewell to Arms* and the myth of Orpheus and Eurydice, to assure possession of the girl is to lose her. Orpheus' art may get him so close to Eurydice that he can bring her back to life, but neither his singing nor his looking can give him possession of her, *alive,* once she has died. We must assume that what Marcel does in his projected novel (and what Proust did in the novel we read) is not to put his "life in Time" accurately into print, but rather to demonstrate to others how *they* have lives in time larger than they had suspected.

Writing, then, is often a way of saving Time for others—readers, characters—at the expense of the reality of the writer's own experience. The autobiographical artist—and in falsifying our memories each of us is an autobiographer—is a kind of Christ. His is the sacrifice that renews time, even as he is intensely aware of death. For to watch one's memories flatten, abstract, and dis-integrate before the falsifying attempts at possession is to become aware of the continual dying of the present, the infinitesimal extent of what-is-real-now. It is possible that repetition in art can turn this infinitesimal into an infinite, but that is for later discussion. The process I have called falsification of reality shows us that we are always dying, that the past is never accessible, even as on-call memory, and is as speculative and "mental" as the future. That we are always dying is the tyranny of the present tense. Personal memory does not, any more than art or children, keep *us* alive. The answer time offers us, and the gift of the present tense, is that we are always living. It is entirely up to us whether our time is always ending or always beginning.

The remainder of this book is devoted to a discussion of constructive repetition. It should become clear that *emphasizing* with near-repetitions does not necessarily free one either from the destructive action of time or from the implications of destructive repetition in that sort of literature which subscribes to the notions of past and future. I use "constructive" in the sense of contributing to the internal power of the work. There are two aesthetics of constructive repetition, differentiated by their attitudes toward memory. The first, involved with the concepts of past and future, and believing in the integrity of memory, builds repetitions one on the other toward some total effect; this "repetition with remembering" takes place in "building time." The second, considering the present the only artistically approachable tense, deals with each instant and subject as a new thing, to such an extent that the sympathetic reader is aware less of repetition than of continuity; this "repetition without remembering" takes place in "continuing time." It is to the discussion of the first of these aesthetics that the following chapter is dedicated.

2. Emphasizing, Echoing, Building, and Complicating

> I have said this now three times. If I were capable, as I wish I were, I could say it once in such a way that it would be there in its complete awefulness. Yet knowing, too, how it is repeated upon each of them, in every day of their lives, so powerfully, so entirely, that it is simply the natural air they breathe, I wonder whether it could ever be said enough times.
>
> —James Agee, *Let Us Now Praise Famous Men*

I have called the time that moves from past to present to future and has history, time that *builds,* and the time that is always present, time that *continues.* In literature and film, these time senses are distinguishable by their uses of repetition. Since this chapter is about building time, it deals necessarily with artists who repeat something *now* to make you remember something *then* and set you up for something that is coming *later;* who build one use of a word on top of another; who draw contrasts and assume you will *remember* how a word was used last and will draw your own conclusions from the difference of context; who *emphasize*. Their art is primarily one of repetition with variation.

From Emphasis to Experience

Throughout *Let Us Now Praise Famous Men*, Agee is trying to say something that cannot be said: he is trying to say life, and the outlet his frustration takes is repetition. He says it three times because he cannot "say it once in such a way that it would be there in its complete awefulness." His only recourse is to insist the audience into his state of mind, to fill them with his frustration at what he cannot say, to repeat his points in an attempt at transforming emphasis into experience: "the natural air they breathe."

This is clearly the limiting case of emphasis. Most outright repetition simply aims to make us remember something, without considering whether accurate human experience is being communicated. Advertising, for example, depends almost entirely on repetition. Where the advertising budget is high, the dedicated television viewer may sit through the same demonstration of the stain-removing power of a certain cleanser or the aphrodisiac marvel of that brunette's toothpaste twenty times in a week. Most of us do not attend to this, but experience it as static; nevertheless many children are growing up singing commercials to themselves.

Propaganda works the same way. It is sometimes harder to turn off.

Fortunately emphasis serves masters other than these communications nightmares, and it is instructive to note how many of those masters defend themselves in advance against the charge of being repetitious. In *Joseph Andrews,* for example, Fielding assures us several times that he does not want to repeat anything unnecessarily:

What the female readers are taught by the memoirs of Mrs. Andrews is so well set forth in the excellent essays or letters prefixed to the second and subsequent editions of that work, that it would be here a needless repetition.[1]

The tone is of course ironic, even suggesting that Richardson's prefixed explanations of *Pamela* were needless repetitions, but his sentence does imply that not all repetitions are needless. Over and over we hear the protestation, "I am more vexed on your account than on my own," we watch the elite manipulate the courts, and we laugh at the dressing-down of affectation. We are shown one character after another who pretends to be higher than humanity—from the lady in the coach who is offended at Joseph's nakedness to the innkeeper's wife who, although unwilling to lose money by helping a dying poor man, professes to be a good

[1] Henry Fielding, *Joseph Andrews,* Book I, Chapter I. Cf. Book I, Chapter 14.

Christian. The characters must frequently choose whether to extend credit to people in need. The juxtaposition of honesty and pretense is repeated as often as the novel will bear, as are the discussions of vanity and charity, virtue, and the role of the clergy.

But Fielding uses repetition for comic as well as didactic effects. It may be that in comedy we expect a character to act the same way most of the time; we feel we see through a character more surely and recognize him faster. So he may be known to us principally through a characterizing joke or costume, which is repeated as often as the character is before us. Mrs. Slipslop's affected speech has real comic vigor at every appearance:

"Yes madam!" replied Mrs. Slipslop with some warmth; "do you intend to *result* my passion? Is it not enough, ungrateful as you are, to make no return to all the favours I have done you; but you must treat me with *ironing?* Barbarous monster! how have I deserved that my passion should be *resulted* and treated with *ironing?*" [2]

This method of characterization through presentation of a repeated trait is of course older than the *commedia dell'arte* and was later used expertly by Dickens and Chekhov, but Fielding is so good at it that I prefer to take the example from him.

Manipulation of repetition for poetic value often de-

[2] *Joseph Andrews,* Book I, Chapter 6.

pends on those "artful" variations that prevent a work from seeming repetitious. Thus the work of Alexander Pope becomes a comedy of symmetry and opposition, as in this line from the *Dunciad:*

> Europe he saw, and Europe saw him too.

One is particularly impressed by the way Pope skirts and maneuvers repetition, like a matador controlling a close pass of the horns. The assumption here is that outright repetition betrays a failure of invention, marking a point where the poem has failed to advance. But repetition is an undeniable source of lyrical strength, as these lines from Milton's *Lycidas* demonstrate:

> But O the heavy change, now thou art gon,
> Now thou art gon, and never must return!

The Old Testament offers us what are at once some of the finest and most familiar examples of the beauty and strength of repetition. Hebrew verse is commonly distinguished from Hebrew prose simply by the bilateral symmetry of its lines; one half of a verse echoes the other:

> Naked came I out of my mother's womb,
> And naked shall I return thither;
> —Job 1:21 [3]

[3] All Old Testament quotations are taken from *The Holy Scriptures* (Philadelphia: Jewish Publication Society, 1917).

Emphasizing, Building, and Complicating

The following verse from Ecclesiastes gives us the sense that when truth is being written about, it can stand being looked at from another direction. Changing the terms only enlarges the reality of the subject, makes the point firmer and more general:

> He that observeth the wind shall not sow;
> And he that regardeth the clouds shall not reap.
> —Ecclesiastes 11:4

In Ecclesiastes and Song of Songs, however, we discover a method of repeating from chapter to chapter that goes beyond simple parallelism. We are familiar in the works of the Prophets with the insistence that makes such a point as "Return, O Jerusalem" many times; we are also used to the sort of inclusiveness that repeats entire histories from I and II Samuel and I and II Kings to I and II Chronicles. Neither are we surprised to find, as a method of characterization, exact repetition of actions within a hero's life: Samson tells his first wife the solution to the strong/sweet riddle and is betrayed by her loyalty to her tribe but triumphs anyway long before he tells Delilah the secret of his strength and is betrayed by her but wins anyway. But the very subject of Ecclesiastes is repetition, and we find not only some of the finest examples of parallelistic verse in that book, but also a deliberate activity of "returning," re-examining a situation until a solution is

39

discovered. We have first the repetition, like a tonic in classical music, of the key phrase:

> Vanity of vanities, saith Koheleth;
> Vanity of vanities, all is vanity. [1:2]

Koheleth's actual poem, which is presented in a prose frame (1:1 and 12:9–13), begins and ends with those words that seal it like a circle, and emphasizes its echoes:

> For all is vanity and a striving after wind. [2:17]
>
> This also is vanity. [2:23]
>
> For childhood and youth are vanity. [11:10]

Observations are repeated in an especially poignant way: Koheleth is pictured as continually *rediscovering* them. He returns—from not considering, or from an unacceptable conclusion, or from the end of the last instant of considering—and considers again.

Wherefore I perceived that there is nothing better, than that a man should rejoice in his works; for that is his portion; for who shall bring him to see what shall be after him?
　But I returned and considered all the oppressions that are done under the sun; and behold the tears of such as were oppressed, and they had no comforter; and on the side of their oppressors there was power, but they had no com-

forter. Wherefore I praised the dead that are already dead more than the living that are yet alive; but better than they both is he that hath not yet been, who hath not seen the evil work that is done under the sun.

Again, I considered all labour and all excelling in work, that it is a man's rivalry with his neighbour. This also is vanity and a striving after wind.

Then I returned and saw vanity under the sun.

[3:22–4:4; 4:7]

The investigation begins again and again. Neither the truth of the observations nor the pain Koheleth feels are mitigated by this persistent re-exploration. These returnings never threaten to become repetitious, because each rediscovery is preceded by a conclusion that, closing the matter for us, frees us to experience each repetition as something new.

In Song of Songs we find a variant of investigative repetition in the verse:

> I rose to open to my beloved;
> And my hands dropped with myrrh,
> And my fingers with flowing myrrh,
> Upon the handles of the bar. [5:5]

The central lines are repeated not only for symmetry in the two halves of the verse; there is emotional reinforcement in the fact that the feeling of flowing was dwelt on, was noticed twice. I am reminded of a scene near the end of Agnes Varda's film *Le Bonheur* (1966), where the shot that shows the husband embracing the drowned body of his wife is repeated many times; the event is coming under scrutiny and is showing itself so large as to find one portrayal insufficient. The husband can't realize what has happened and goes into a kind of temporal shock; repeating the scene signifies the intensity of his observation and emotion. At the same time, the director is looking hard at this moral crisis, so that the repeated shot both communicates the husband's pain and calls the audience's attention to the ambiguity and importance of the embrace.

Finally, Song of Songs is laced with recurring situations, recurring arguments—most notably the several searchings in the night by the woman for the man, and the punctuating:

> I adjure you, O daughters of Jerusalem,
> By the gazelles, and by the hinds of the field,
> That ye awaken not, nor stir up love,
> Until it please. [3:5] [4]

[4] In *The New English Bible* this verse has an entirely different interpretation, but still serves in a sense to punctuate the poem. It is now considered to be spoken by the bridegroom, and to read:

> I charge you, daughters of Jerusalem,
> by the gazelles and the hinds of the field:
> Do not rouse her, do not disturb my love
> until she is ready. [Or, "while she is resting"]
>   [New York: Cambridge University Press, 1971]

This particular verse operates in much the same way as the refrain in a ballad. It makes a point of which the entire story is an illustration; even if we cannot really understand the full relevance of the moral until we have heard the whole story, we are kept to a definite viewpoint throughout the rendition. We attach new material to the refrain as it comes to us, as we would clip a sail to a mast.

Thus throughout "The Barring of the Door"—a ballad about an old couple who so stubbornly keep to a pact of silence that they allow their house to be ransacked by highwaymen before the old man speaks out—and loses the pact, and has to bar the door—the refrain reminds us that the keystone to this story is "the barring of our door well." In "Lord Randal," an exchange of dialogue between a mother and her son, who was poisoned by eating eels while hunting, verges on the absurd as the mother asks questions and the son answers her, interjecting each time:

". . . mother, mak my bed soon,
For I'm sick at the heart, and I fain wad lie down." [5]

It is not even necessary that Randal die in this ballad; we got the point long before. But his dying is not the point of the ballad in any case. The importance of this

[5] Child 12A, in Sargent and Kittredge, eds., *English and Scottish Popular Ballads,* Cambridge Edition (Boston & New York: Houghton Mifflin Co., 1904), p. 22.

exchange, we find, is in the juxtaposition of the urgency of Randal's sickness and the decisions he makes about what to leave to whom. This is a juxtaposition whose repetition in each stanza does not exhaust itself all the way to the resolution, where Randal leaves his castle to his mother, his money to his sister, his real estate to his brother, and:

"What d'ye leave to your true-love, Lord Randal, my son?
What d'ye leave to your true-love, my handsome young man?"
"I leave her hell and fire; mother, mak my bed soon,
For I'm sick at the heart, and I fain wad lie down."

The true-love, of course, is the one who cooked him the eels. A ballad can be considered resolved when the changing material at the head of each verse reaches the solidity of the unchanging refrain: when novelty touches repetition. When their lines have equal confidence and completion, the two halves of the form have come together. Real resolution in a ballad, then, comes about not when the story-line is satisfied—that is one way the changing line itself is internally resolved—but when the two formal elements are of equal strength, when the changing attains the *being* of the fixed.

Movement in "Lord Randal" is between the near-still and the nearer-still.[6] If we see the interest in

[6] The refrain, of course, does alter in context; it is received differently depending on how much the listener has learned at

change and "things of this world" as Western (vanity) and the interest in the unchanging and "movements without motion" (as in the *Tao Tê Ching*) as Eastern, then we may find in the ballad an archetype that educates us by leading us out of the illusion of the importance of change. The Hindu concept of *samsara* reminds us that the "sorrow and impurity of the world" [7] is a delusion and vanity. We educate ourselves out of it in many ways, one of which is the chanting of a repetitive poem or *mantra*. This pure repetition charms the mind, and allows it to see past the illusion of change to the truth (unity). The two lines of the ballad also conform to two differing notions of time: time that has history, and time that tends to move only in the present. The role of repetition as a deliverer from history, and ultimately from time—a power it reveals in the mantra —is taken up in the final chapters of this book.

Refrain is the spine of the ballad. Other poetic devices, which do not persist so emphatically but still introduce elements of repetition into literature, are

---

the end of each verse about the story. There are many near-repetitions in the "changing" line (in each verse, Randal is asked twice what he will leave to the subject of that verse; and the act of inquiring repeats in every verse), and many contextual developments in the "unchanging" line (which may, in fact, change its text, as at the end of "The Elfin Knight"). Let us say that the "unchanging" line is *nearer* to repetition.

[7] Joseph Campbell, *The Masks of God: Oriental Mythology* (New York: Viking Press, 1962), p. 351.

rhyme and alliteration. Both could have applied to
them the definition Whitehead gave rhythm: "a fusion
of sameness and novelty." All three tend to unify, even
when used uninventively,[8] for the repetition of sound,
no matter what its "meaning," is the glue of poetry.
Used well, these techniques are rarely monotonous
("repetitious").

Here is a different instance of repetition's power to
emphasize a point: Sergei Eisenstein's formulation of a
theory of film editing.

By what, then, is montage characterized and, consequently,
its cell—the shot?

By collision. By the conflict of two pieces in opposition
to each other. By conflict. By collision.[9]

The Russian director's prose here offers a clue to his
manner of emphasis in film. Eisenstein not only builds
his montage out of the dialectical juxtaposition of con-
flicting shots, but also repeats parts of scenes, starting
over and stretching time for emphasis. In *October* [*Ten
Days that Shook the World*, 1927], there is a powerful
scene in which a crowd attempting to cross a draw-
bridge is machine-gunned and the bridge is raised. A
dead woman is lifted with one half of the bridge, a

[8] Compare rock's primordial rhyming of "love" with "of"—
not much resonance, but it's definitely song.

[9] Sergei Eisenstein, *Film Form*, trans. Jan Leyda (New York:
Harcourt, Brace & Co., 1949), p. 37.

horse and carriage with the other. The dead horse and the long hair of the woman, each hanging over the bridge-edges, repeat each other graphically. The sections of the bridge begin to rise, begin to rise again, rise, and rise, until the bridge-halves are vertical, the woman slides back, the horse falls from his shafts into the river, and the carriage crashes to the base of the bridge. As the hanging horse and hair is a repetition in composition, the rebegun bridge-raising is a repetition in time. This is a scene that begins the viewer in it again as it begins again.[10] We find a similar expansion of space and time in Eisenstein's earlier *Potemkin* (1925), where in the Odessa steps sequence a mother's body falls against her baby's carriage and the carriage starts to move three times before it actually carries the child down the steps to his death. We remember also the rhythmic alternation of the shots of the soldiers' advancing with their guns, marching down the steps, and firing, with the shots of fleeing citizens. The actual number of steps separating the soldiers from the people can be seen to be descended many times over, if one can detach himself from the extraordinary sequence long enough to count.

Eisenstein's montage transfigures many techniques in

[10] This seems to me to be the exact effect of the lines from Song of Songs: "And my hands dropped with myrrh, / And my fingers with flowing myrrh." The hands are noticed twice, and thus in a sense *occur* twice in the work; the effect of this repetition is to enlarge our experience of time, to begin us again.

addition to repetition; yet it is possible to relate his theory of editing to V. I. Pudovkin's (conventionally considered its alternative) on the basis of the two directors' conceptions of repetition.

If Eisenstein's use of repetition in conflict-montage may be called *expressive,* that of his great contemporary, Pudovkin—who believed shots should analogically complement one another—may be called *didactic.*[11] Writing about D. W. Griffith's *Way Down East,* for example, Pudovkin particularly praised the way a snowstorm repeated and clarified the "storm" in the heroine's heart.[12] In Pudovkin's masterpiece, *Mother* (1926), there are many instances of parallel, rather than dialectical, montage, of which the most famous is the crosscutting of a protest march with a river in thaw. Though his concern remained with problems of emphasis, Pudovkin was aware also of the effectiveness of outright repetition of entire sequences, as he makes clear in this discussion of a screenplay submitted to his studio:

Often it is interesting for the scenarist especially to emphasize the basic theme of the scenario. For this purpose exists the method of reiteration. Its nature can easily be demonstrated by an example. In an anti-religious scenario

[11] Of course I am speaking only of those of their montages that used repetition; it doesn't seem reasonable to consider *all* conflict-montage "expressive repetition."

[12] V. I. Pudovkin, *Film Technique,* trans. Ivor Montagu (London: George Newnes, Ltd., 1935), p. 101.

48

that aimed at exposing the cruelty and hypocrisy of the Church in employ of the Tsarist régime the same shot was several times repeated: a church-bell slowly ringing and, superimposed upon it, the title: "The sound of bells sends into the world a message of patience and love." This piece appeared whenever the scenarist desired to emphasize the stupidity of patience, or the hypocrisy of the love thus preached.[13]

Another way of saying that repetition emphasizes is to say that it *makes intense and solid through persistence.*[14] Repeated enough, a word or idea or phrase or

[13] *Ibid.*, pp. 49–50.

[14] This seems to be the sort of emphasis attempted in one of the greatest repetition films, *Yoko Ono Number Four* (1966): a ninety-minute succession, in black and white, of nude human buttocks walking away from the camera while they are on a treadmill and the camera is fixed—giving the impression of walking in place, or of four gray areas shifting in relation to each other—about twenty seconds per person. The first five minutes seem very long (and it is at this point that most of the audience leaves), but soon the extraordinary quality of the visual repetition itself takes hold, and the remainder of the film seems to take place very quickly. *Number Four* can be a revelatory humanistic experience, or an exercise in abstraction, but whether one attends to the four abstract, shifting areas or the spectacle of humanity—not to mention the clever soundtrack: a montage of the rationalizations for or against taking part in the film, recorded in the room adjoining that in which the filming was taking place, and spoken by the hundreds of Londoners who answered an ad for "intellectual bottoms"—one is readily convinced of the reality and importance of what at first seems an uninteresting subject.

image or name will come to dominate us to such an extent that our only defenses are to concede its importance or turn off the stimulus completely. Here the art consists in carrying the audience along in phase with the build of the repetitions—dominating the audience and relaxing the build just before it becomes unbearable.[15]

Nevertheless, emphasis is nearly always expressive of frustration at the inadequacy of the simple statement to convey experience—that is, to give one the sense of having experienced the truth. We can only hint at what we cannot say—can only emphasize until emphasis itself communicates. John Donne's Sermon LXXVII, from the Folio of 1640, dares to express our sense of the inexpressible; its method is repetition.

"It is a fearful thing to fall into the hands of the living God"; but to fall out of the hands of the living God is a horror beyond our expression, beyond our imagination.

. . . that this God at last should let this soul go away as a smoke, as a vapor, as a bubble; and that then this soul cannot be a smoke, a vapor, nor a bubble but must lie in dark-

[15] Still, experience is largely a matter of bearing the unbearable, of moving with the overwhelming; persistence past the conventional point of saturation can result in communications of an almost extraliterary sort. Most readers find Gertrude Stein incomprehensible because she has rejected "build"; her repetitions strike them as a barrage, a frequency that perhaps her little dog could hear, but that they cannot. Of course it seems "unbearable" precisely because they *expect* her to build.

ness as long as the Lord of light is light itself, and never spark of that light reach to my soul; what Tophet is not paradise, what brimstone is not amber, what gnashing is not a comfort, what gnawing of the worm is not a tickling, what torment is not a marriage-bed to this damnation, to be secluded eternally, eternally, eternally from the sight of God? [16]

This wholly different kind of hell is insisted into existence. The only way Donne could possibly cap such a build is with direct insistent re-use of the same word: eternally, eternally, eternally. Here we may compare Faulkner's *Absalom, Absalom!*, whose characters are driven, in their attempts to evoke the reality of Thomas Sutpen, to furious outpourings of involuted rhetoric, and which can end, in frenzied ambiguity, only with repetition: " 'I dont hate it . . . I dont hate it,' he said. *I dont hate it* he thought . . . *I dont. I dont! I dont hate it! I dont hate it!*" When the subject is beyond direct expression, what one builds with is almost less important to the emotional communication than the fact that one is building. No single word can contain this urgency; the word must be used so that the urgency speaks through it. When Lear cried, "Howl, howl, howl!" his language was attempting to transcend lan-

[16] Text from Witherspoon and Warnke, *Seventeenth-Century Prose and Poetry*, 2d ed. (New York: Harcourt, Brace & World, 1963), p. 105. The sentence excerpted here is over four hundred words in length.

guage, entering a world where the emphasis of "Never, never, never, never, never" was inadequate to convey "never." Filled as it is with echoes and doubles, *King Lear* may serve by itself as a laboratory in the uses of constructive repetition.

King Lear

Perhaps the first thing one notices about *King Lear* is the way certain words return, often in different contexts, and the larger working-out of this technique in the presence of a subplot that varies and amplifies but virtually repeats the main plot. Sometimes it seems as if most of the people on stage are projections of Lear—notably the Fool, who appears and disappears without warning in that part of the play where Lear's mental stability is in question, and Gloucester, who even after seeing how Lear is deceived by Goneril and Regan and how he turns against his honest Cordelia is himself deceived by Edmund and turns against the innocent Edgar. Gloucester's physical blindness repeats on a less tragic level Lear's lack of insight. The innocent Edgar's adaptability contrasts with the innocent Cordelia's rigidity. Goneril, Regan, and Edmund "all marry in an instant." Lear's and Edmund's invocations of Nature as their goddess call attention to each other. Kent and Gloucester and Cornwall's three servants are models of loyal service, set respectively against Oswald, Cornwall, and—in so far as Cornwall's first servant, attempting to stop his master from doing evil, is a variant of Kent—Oswald again. We are made aware of the difference between characters when those we would not ordinarily think of in terms of each other act out similar scenes in different ways, as when France makes Cordelia his, and Cornwall makes Edmund his, with similar words—the one a meeting of the virtuous, the other a meeting of the vicious:

FRANCE: Fairest Cordelia, that art most rich being poor,
  Most choice forsaken, and most loved despised,
  Thee and thy virtues here I seize upon. [1.1]

CORNWALL: For you, Edmund,
  Whose virtue and obedience doth this instant
  So much commend itself, you shall be ours.
  Natures of such deep trust we shall much need;
  You we first seize on. [2.1]

The success of this allusive technique requires that the audience have the entire play in its head throughout the performance, for the play reflects itself at every turn and makes most of its moral points by this calling attention to difference. (Similarly, we experience the problems of action, vengeance, and succession in *Hamlet* in great depth as a result of being able to compare, in Fortinbras, Laertes, and Hamlet, three variants of its unintegrated hero.)

53

We become aware not simply of the differences between characters but also of the complex interrelations and implications of the play's themes through the repetition of key words and images. We may take "dark" as an example, simply because there isn't room to examine the omnipresent "nature."

Lear, announcing his intention to divide his kingdom, says, "Meantime we shall express our darker purpose" (1.1). He means "hidden," but "darker" strikes the tonic of a theme that is developed through every association of blindness, evil, and folly of which metaphoric condensation in this play is capable. Lear's fault in the first scene is of irresponsibility and lack of insight. He does "wrong" (1.5) and "evil" (1.1). When Goneril "asks" him to give up half his knights, Lear cries, "Darkness and devils!" (1.4). Addressing the Gloucester she is later to help blind, Regan hints:

> Thus out of season, threading dark-eyed night,
> Occasions, noble Gloucester, of some prize,
> Wherein we must have use of your advice. [2.1]

There is some echo to this night visit in Kent's lines, during the storm:

> The wrathful skies
> Gallow the very wanderers of the dark
> And make them keep their caves. [3.2]

Edgar, as Poor Tom, tells Lear in the same breath that he broke oaths and "did the act of darkness" with his mistress (3.4). He continues this emphasis with the conventional yet transfigured, "The prince of darkness is a gentleman." Blinded, Gloucester cries, "All dark and comfortless," and sees the vengeance he expects Edmund to execute as light ("sparks of nature"—3.7). Finally the link between Lear's lack of insight and Gloucester's blindness, and between the darkness of sin and error and that of their attendant punishments, is forged with Edgar's words:

> The gods are just, and of our pleasant vices
> Make instruments to plague us.
> The dark and vicious place where thee he got
> Cost him his eyes. [5.3]

Obviously "dark" now carries the resonance that a playfull of interrelated usages has given it.

Entire lines as well as words can call attention to each other, as in the paralleled "seizings" of Cordelia by France and of Edmund by Cornwall. The most clearcut example of such a parallel follows:

> LEAR: . . . what can you say to draw
> A third more opulent than your sisters? Speak.
> CORDELIA: Nothing, my lord. [1.1]

GLOUCESTER: What paper were you reading?
EDMUND: Nothing, my lord. [1.2]

The ironic contrast between Cordelia's honesty and Edmund's deceit is made even more obvious than their actions make it, by this virtual repetition of an exchange.

But the repetitions for which *Lear* is most famous are those direct successions of words by the identical words, which give the dialogue its authentic tone of madness, frustration, and grief.

LEAR: I'll put't in proof,
And when I have stolen upon these son-in-laws,
Then kill, kill, kill, kill, kill, kill! [4.6]

Lear's madness takes away the space between his words. Edmund's "bastardy" outburst is the first of these driven lines. We see that "base" obsesses him, that he is anxious about it, the more he asserts the advantages of bastardy. The word melts before us into Edmund's very personal meanings for it, even as Edmund's baseness is impressed upon us:

Why bastard? Wherefore base,
When my dimensions are as well compact,
My mind as generous, and my shape as true,
As honest madam's issue? Why brand they us
With base? with baseness? Bastardy base? Base? [1.2]

Lear's repeating is the principal way Shakespeare expresses the old man's madness and pain. Again, what is beyond our expression is most forcefully put in a syntax of pure emphasis.

LEAR: And my poor fool is hanged: no, no, no life?
    Why should a dog, a horse, a rat, have life,
    And thou no breath at all? Thou'lt come no more,
    Never, never, never, never, never.
    Pray you undo this button. Thank you, sir.
    Do you see this? Look on her! Look her lips,
    Look there, look there— [5.3]

To summarize the many uses of repetition in *King Lear:* There is the succession of identical words either to transcend language (Howl, howl, howl!) or to bring out that word's special poetic nature (Lurk, lurk).

There is the repetition of similar-sounding lines that suggest each other and call attention to their differences, as the following three lines bind and morally interilluminate their speakers and their points:

LEAR: So young, and so untender?
CORDELIA: So young, my lord, and true. [1.1]

REGAN: So white, and such a traitor? [3.7]

There is the exact repetition of words in different contexts, which we are thus forced to interrelate. When

Lear enters with the dead Cordelia in his arms, Kent asks whether this is the promised end (of the play, of the world), and Edgar answers him in words which directly echo Edmund's:

EDMUND: Brother, I advise you to the best. Go armed. I am no honest man if there be any good meaning toward you. I have told you what I have seen and heard; but faintly, nothing like the image and horror of it. [1.2]

KENT: Is this the promised end?
EDGAR: Or image of that horror? [5.3]

There is the basic repetition of parallel plots, and corollary to that, the repetition of certain kinds of confrontation. Thus the onslaught of "Who's there?" in Acts One and Three continually calls the audience's attention to the related problems of nature, disguise, allegiance, and honesty.

Most demandingly, there are those words that carry the meanings they have acquired in earlier contexts with them into their present and future contexts, immensely complicating and interrelating the concerns and actions of the play, and pointing solutions within the play to its problems:

GLOUCESTER: . . . and the bond cracked 'twixt son and father. [1.2]

GLOUCESTER: O madam, my old heart is cracked, it's cracked. [2.1]

LEAR: Crack Nature's moulds, all germains spill at once, That makes ingrateful man. [3.1]

EDGAR: His grief grew puissant, and the strings of life Began to crack. [5.3]

LEAR: Had I your tongues and eyes, I'd use them so That heaven's vault should crack. She's gone for ever. [5.3]

Here the familial and elemental catastrophes that befall Lear and Gloucester are firmly associated with the violation of natural ties, Lear's change in attitude toward his natural bond to Cordelia is ironically emphasized, and the contrast between Gloucester's passivity and Lear's rebellious rage is drawn from among these uses of the word "crack."

Miracle of the Rose

Jean Genet's novelized reminiscence, *Miracle of the Rose,* is as much about the falsification of reality as it is about any of its other subjects: prison routine, the transcendent beauty of crime, homosexual love, religion. It is also an outstanding example of the generation of a mystical symbol through the artful manipulation of repetition. Genet weaves his present in one prison into his past in others and his past loves into his present. He does not so much repeat specific incidents as he dwells on similar situations; the swings between the prisons Fontevrault and Mettray, and between the lovers Bulkaen and Divers, repeat so often as to form the dominant texture of the work. By dwelling on his loves, Genet discovers that their reality is being transformed into art, but instead of finding this upsetting, he glories in it. The revelation of immortal beauty becomes a main theme.

He spoke again at great length about Villeroy, but a surprising thing happened: as he went on talking, the image I had retained of my big shot grew dimmer instead of clearer. Divers adorned him with qualities of which I was unaware. He referred several times to his powerful arms. Now, Villeroy had very ordinary arms. Finally he dwelt on the way he dressed and then on his member, which he said must have been something special since he had won and kept me. Gradually the old image of Villeroy gave way to another one, a stylized one.[17]

Genet tells the story of his loves and illuminations over and over, and each time we come closer to a real under-

[17] Jean Genet, *Miracle of the Rose,* trans. Bernard Frechtman (New York: Grove Press, 1967), pp. 157–158. Copyright © 1966 by Grove Press, Inc. Copyright © 1951 and 1965 by Jean Genet. Translation copyright © 1965 by Anthony Blond Limited. This and other quotations from this translation are reprinted by permission of Grove Press, Inc.

standing of that (stylized) reality. We are in a painful but art-transformed world. The more Genet talks or hears about his lovers and prisons, the more stylized they become to him and the more definite in his work: the more real to us. The falsification of reality is, to him, part of the transcendent character of art.

The story of Genet's loves is balanced by the continually returned-to story of Harcamone, a prisoner whose execution closes the novel. Harcamone is an existential saint. Where the reality of Bulkaen and other mortals is transformed upward into art, stylized by and into a greater force, the reality of Harcamone is greater than that of art; the novel must strain all bounds—dwell again and again in a science of pain and detail on the past and the present, the mortal and the immortal, the emotional and the impossible—in an attempt to touch the reality of Harcamone. As narration transforms the lesser characters, Harcamone transforms the novel. "Falsification of reality" operates on an entirely lower plane than Harcamone's. Dwelling on his encounters with Harcamone, Genet does sometimes experience that fading of the accurate image discussed in our last chapter; but it is only the memory of the encounter that is smothered. Harcamone's reality, which stylizes art up to *its* level, cannot be undermined: "Words have no power over Harcamone's image. They will not exhaust it, for its matter is inexhaustible." [18] But what language

[18] *Ibid.,* p. 246.

cannot exhaust, it has difficulty describing. Throughout the novel Genet tells us how painful it is for him to say anything at all. Harcamone is beyond the reach of words even as he is beyond their harm. "If I take leave of this book," Genet concludes, "I take leave of what can be related. The rest is ineffable." [19]

Genet's novel dedicates itself to the capture, in language, of one complex living moment: the incarnation of mystic criminal saintly beauty in Harcamone, in a vision Genet has while lying with an old lover on the night of Harcamone's execution: a vision in which Harcamone's judge, lawyer, chaplain, and executioner, abruptly the size of bedbugs, enter Harcamone's mouth and search for the heart of his heart; in the deepest chamber a door opens *by itself* and reveals "a red rose of monstrous size and beauty." Much of the aim of the novel is to prepare a climate for the rose to reveal itself —to create a mood of the ineffable. The miracle of the rose is pursued not "in time" but in an anti-temporal labyrinth—built up to in a three-hundred-page architecture of interrelations, investigations, flashbacks, and visions. Without actually repeating any scenes, the novel builds up a tremendous tension as the repetitive *pattern of transition* proceeds. We feel by the end of the work that we have experienced one moment, but we are not sure which one: it is an experience that refracts eternity.

[19] *Ibid.,* p. 344.

Genet manipulates the reader's progress through this epiphany with his near-repetitions:

To speak of saintliness again in connection with transportation will set your teeth on edge, for they are not used to an acid diet.[20]

The clue to Genet's anti-mask emerges when Genet discusses how Harcamone killed a guard:

Since he avoided repetition, he was less aware of sinking into misfortune, for all too often people overlook the suffering of the murderer who always kills in the same way (Wiedman and his bullet in the back of the neck, etc.), since it is most painful to invent a new and difficult gesture.[21]

Repetition, then, makes us aware of our position; in this case it is associated with a suffering of which most outsiders are unaware. Yet even as Harcamone discovers he *has* sunk into misfortune, by the end of this repetitive work we as readers feel the immense power of the rose apotheosis from having consciously or unconsciously gotten close to it so often. Even though the miracle of the rose itself occurs only once, we have had our teeth "set on edge" many times by the incidents and assumptions that anticipate it—the prison as a mystic com-

[20] *Ibid.*, p. 45.   [21] *Ibid.*, pp. 61–62.

munity, bullets as flowers, chains as garlands—and the rose has taken on that quality of transcendent mystery which E. K. Brown identifies with the expanding symbol in the work of Proust and Forster.

Brown's essential thesis, which applies to Genet's novel quite as well as it did to Brown's original subject, *A Passage to India,* reads:

To express what is both an order and a mystery rhythmic processes, repetitions with intricate variations, are the most appropriate of idioms. Repetition is the strongest assurance an author can give of order; the extraordinary complexity of the variations is the reminder that the order is so involute that it must remain a mystery.[22]

Such an analysis poses problems of its own: the ineffable is not merely complicated. Certainly the symbol of the rose takes on greater meaning, and its sense of being "both an order and a mystery," through just such a use of repetition with variation. But *Miracle of the Rose* gives a sense of something beyond the involute. As I shall attempt to show in the next chapter, it is repetition, and not its complications, that tends to involve itself in the concept and experience of eternity. I would like to conclude this chapter with a brief consideration

[22] E. K. Brown, *Rhythm in the Novel* (Toronto: University of Toronto Press, and London: Oxford University Press, 1950), p. 115.

of pornography and the horror film, through which I hope to make this tendency to timelessness clear.

Pornography and the Horror Film

As R. H. W. Dillard has pointed out,[23] the great danger in the horror film is the failure of death. Wolf Man, mummy, zombie, or vampire, the undead are doomed to rise from their graves and continue a parody of life forever. Unable to die, they are doomed to repetition. The sequel thus becomes a perfect expression of the threat, situation, and plight of the horror object.

Most horror sequels simply extend the situation of their original; all the Frankenstein films, for example, are linked—the beginning of each sequel explains away the death that occurred in the previous film. The Dracula films, on the other hand, honor the death of the original Count but produce his relatives and victims, one after the other, as fresh "draculas." Such sequels demonstrate the popularity of the formulaic more than the power of repetition. One sequel-series, however, does deal in genuine repetition, and it deserves serious consideration here.

The Mummy (1932) differs considerably from its sequels. The mummy, here called Imhotep—Kharis in

[23] R. H. W. Dillard, "Even a Man Who Is Pure at Heart: Poetry and Danger in the Horror Film," in *Man and the Movies,* ed. W. R. Robinson (Baltimore: Penguin, 1969).

the sequels—attempts to bring his dead love, the Princess Anckesenamon, back to life, and is punished by the gods; later he attempts to reincarnate the princess in a living girl, and is punished again. The sequels to this film begin on new ground.

The Mummy's Hand (1940), *The Mummy's Tomb* (1942), *The Mummy's Ghost* (1944), and *The Mummy's Curse* (1945) are nearly indistinguishable. The burning Tana leaves, the dragging leg, and the consistent motivation of the mummy—under all those bandages we remember the princess's lover, as we watch this parody of his defiance of death—do not change. In each version the priest controlling Kharis attempts to make the heroine immortal like Kharis and flirts, to his own destruction, with the idea of making himself immortal with her; it is this particular plot element whose recurrence makes the mummy sequels feel more like repetitions, or variations on a theme, than the string of deaths and resurrections undergone by the Frankenstein monster and the Wolf Man. The series even has a happy ending, one which is very important for our purposes. In *The Mummy's Ghost* the princess (now "Ananka") is reincarnated in a living girl (cf. *The Mummy*) when Kharis attempts to embrace Ananka's mummy in a California museum, where it is on exhibit. From the moment of this spiritual transfer, the living girl begins to age. Finally, Kharis takes the girl away from the priest who has gone through the "Shall I make myself immortal with her" routine and walks into quicksand. With every cut from the pursuing vigilantes and the girl's American lover back to Kharis, we see her older, until the two lovers, equally old, are united in death. It is interesting to note that this successful ending was initiated by Kharis' attempt to embrace the real and original Ananka: that this attempt at reuniting with the primary love object failed in itself, but made possible a resolution with a new Ananka, a live woman who had aged, a *rebegun* mummy. Clearly this film was made not to have a sequel, and only the demands of the box office, the popularity of the mummy as a cinematic image, and the essential pleasure of repetition, can explain the release of the later *Mummy's Curse*.

The mummy films did not exhaust themselves in the search for novelty which weakened and misled the Frankenstein series. The mummy's image, motive, and machinery do not change; a full-fledged myth is allowed to reappear with all its intrinsic force. Whatever variations do occur, usually in the identity and location of the victims and priests, do not upstage the central figure and are in harmony with his story.

The compulsive variation associated with the circumstances of sexual encounter in pornography may reflect an aesthetic problem rather than a sexual one. An artist who cannot make repetition interesting in itself, or who cannot project urgency and force into his *writing* of the sex act, may rely on novelty. Pornography *must* not bore. Since pornography conventionally regards plot as an occasion only for varying the circumstances and position of intercourse, and is interested more in portraying sex than in relating it to anything else or exploring its implications, this literature more than any other is faced with the difficulty of making repetition aesthetically viable. The usual technique is to avoid exactly repeating encounters by complicating positions, changing the number of participants, and intensifying the adjectives (repetition with variation). This reliance on extreme variation proceeds from insecurity; it reflects both the artist's lack of faith in his material and in his ability to present it in its own strength, and the audience's fear of personalized demanding relationships. Repetition means confrontation. Novelties of partner and position keep writer and reader from the realities of repetition relationships: that person who is still there, that complex and personal need, that intense continuity. Novelty is essential to the pornographic illusion of uncommitted and instantaneous, always exciting but never confronted sex. It is possible that pornography's audience has been conditioned to expect extreme changes of partner and technique by the pornographer's inadequate response to his artistic problem—how to keep intercourse interesting in this work, or how to *justify* the basic repetition— rather than by listening to its own sexual inclinations. In any case, their insecurities serve each other.

According to Steven Marcus, the ideal pornographic novel would repeat forever—"it would have no ending, just as in pornotopia there is ideally no such thing as time."[24] Repetitions in pornography do not lead to gratification, an end to pleasure; as noted in my discussion of Freud and Kubie, no neurotic, compulsive repetition will be able to resolve itself through repetition alone ("No compulsive work drive has ever healed itself through working"). Even though the pornographer does stoop to novelty in an effort to make his "novel" interesting, the repetition of the essential pornographic situation itself shows through these pseudo-artistic variations. Here, at the ground zero of pornography, the unchanging anonymous sexual urge is conveyed by simple repeating words: again, again, again; more, more, more.[25] These words are experienced as facts; they repeat because the motions of intercourse repeat, conveying rhythm more than meaning, allowing the audience to read in its own tension. This shows through all the variation, and is an example of a repeated word's transcending its literal meaning. Repetition is a vehicle to timelessness, and to what Wittgenstein called "the mystical." The conscientious pornographer takes masturbation for his mantra.

Those horror-film sequels whose heroes are undead

[24] Steven Marcus, *The Other Victorians* (New York: Basic Books, 1966), p. 279.
[25] *Ibid.*

tend also, in repetition, to go on forever. For them too there is ideally no sense of time. From *The Mummy's Ghost* we learn that one of the only ways to stop something that if left to itself will repeat forever is to present it with a repetition in opposition to its repetitions: a repetition in reverse. (This aesthetic variant of transference psychology is most clearly worked out in Yeats's *Purgatory,* which will be discussed in the next chapter.) But if one is concerned less with reasserting the values of a threatened clock-time society than with discovering a new life outside time for one's consciousness and one's literature, one might put off his mummy- and book-burning and turn to a serious examination of that timelessness that repetition has so often been used to convey. A work might go on forever as a means of directing us to what is forever. Repetition contains within itself the germ of the nature of eternity; and eternity is not "a long time"—it is timeless.

3. Eternity in an Hour

I am content to live it all again
And yet again, if it be life . . .
—W. B. Yeats, *A Dialogue of Self and Soul* [1]

Some of the aesthetic problems of sequels and pornography are relevant in helping us to make the transition from considerations of building time to those of
continuing time. There are many works of twentieth-
century literature that contain no recognizable system
of time-counting, whose final sentences bleed into their
first, that expand infinitely or infinitesimally. Often in
such works a repetition will be employed not to build
on our memory of what it repeats, but as if this were
the first time we had seen it and it were necessary to
insist on the subject's existence, to rebegin the discussion just as each frame of a film rebegins the entire
screen image. This chapter will concern itself with those

[1] Reprinted with permission of The Macmillan Company
from *Selected Poems and Two Plays of William Butler Yeats*, ed.
M. L. Rosenthal, p. 125. Copyright 1933 by The Macmillan Company, renewed 1961 by Bertha Georgie Yeats. Reprinted also
with permission of Mr. M. B. Yeats and Macmillan & Co. Ltd.
from *Collected Poems of W. B. Yeats*.

works that exist on the margins of both time-systems, whose characters move both in time and in eternity.

Repetition in Reverse: Purgatory, The Blacks, and The Exterminating Angel

In W. B. Yeats's last play, *Purgatory*, both the living and the dead, the material and the spiritual, the objective and the subjective appear at once on one stage. An Old Man brings his son to the ruins of a burned-out house, the Old Man's birthplace. He explains that the Boy's grandmother had made an impulsive marriage to a groom and died in childbirth. The groom had squandered her money, cut down the trees, "killed" and finally burned down the house. In that fire, which occurred when the Old Man was sixteen, the Old Man stabbed his drunken father and fled. He had had a classical education, but gave none to the Boy—who in fact shares some of the grandfather's amoral materialistic coarseness and, hearing the story, approves of his grandfather's actions. Applying Yeats's gyre-distinctions to character, we can recognize the Old Man as subjective, his father and son objective, and the ghost of his mother in a state of enforced inter-incarnational subjectivity.

The Old Man hints to the Boy that the mother's ghost still lives in that house, which must be the site of her purgation. We gather from his presentation that the mother's sin was her lust for the drunken groom, which was the first cause of the ruin of her house and the cause of the Old Man's existence (and with that existence, or "pollution," his act of parricide). She must endure many dream repetitions of her wedding night until she understands her sin, or until God frees her from this trap, or until living people help her to "end the consequence" of her sin. Others may help end the consequences "upon others"; but where the consequence touches the sufferer, the dream repeats until the sufferer understands his transgression himself, or is released by God.[2] The Old Man attempts to help his mother's soul by ending the consequence her transgression might have upon others, by making sure that no more offspring come indirectly from her marriage. While the Old Man and Boy are on stage, the mother's dream begins: the groom's hoofbeats are heard, the mother's silhouette appears in the house, and the two ghosts repeat the begetting of the Old Man. The Old Man hears the dream immediately, perhaps from his subjective bias; the Boy neither hears the approaching ghost-horse nor sees the young girl in the lighted window. He brings the Old Man's attention back to the world of the living, and simultaneously the light in the window fades out, suggesting that the audience's perception of the mother's repeating dream is dependent on the Old Man's perception of it—or that the dream is directed at the Old Man—or perhaps that it is the Old Man's dream. The

2 See W. B. Yeats, *Purgatory,* lines 33–42 (Rosenthal, p. 203).

Boy attempts to steal the Old Man's money. They fight. The window lights up. The Boy realizes that he and the Old Man are about to re-enact, in the present, the confrontation which had ended in parricide (the Old Man was sixteen when he killed his father; the Boy in the play is sixteen); and now the Boy sees the silhouette in the window. He is involved in the dream. He has taken the roles both of the Old Man (sixteen-year-old would-be parricide) and of the father (objective opposed to subjective; avenger and moral approver of his grandfather). The audience is set for a repetition of the parricide: a reliving of the dream both upstage and downstage: a continuation of the sin. What occurs, however, is not that the Boy kills the Old Man, takes the money, and in getting children passes "pollution on"—but that the Old Man kills the Boy. The window grows dark.

This ends the first repetition of the dream—a dream that has involved living characters. The Old Man has repeated his own crime: he has killed two blood relatives with the same knife on the same spot. He has "finished" the consequence upon others of his mother's marriage, he thinks, in that there will be no more children. But the dream begins again: we and the Old Man hear the hoofbeats. The Old Man concludes that he— "others"—has exhausted his possibilities of helping his mother; returning to the terms in which he originally described the condition of purgatory, he finds that the repetitions must continue until the mother understands the consequence upon herself, or until God intervenes.

Now if only the mother were in purgatory, this conclusion would be valid; and it may be that the mother's more subjective repeating is on a different level from the Old Man's. But it is hard to overlook the fact that the Old Man himself has returned to the site of *his* crime, that he kills his son in the same place with the same knife, that we do not see him leave the house at the end of the play and we did not see him arrive at the beginning. He seems to be in an earthly version of his own definition of purgatory. In the play's last line he asks that both he and his mother be allowed to find peace; this may literally suggest that the terms of his purgatory-metaphysic apply both to himself and to his mother. We are led to conclude that the mother has not realized the consequence of her transgression on herself—but isn't it obvious that neither has the Old Man, who defends his parricide and filicide throughout, recognized the consequence of his transgressions on himself? Isn't it clear that both of them need to relive their transgressions until they come to this awareness or until God gives peace? The temporal and the atemporal are joined by repetition. The subjective (ghost) and objective (living) gyres are locked in phase.

Since the metaphysics of purgatory are conveyed to us by the Old Man, by the Boy's gradual involvement in the dream, and by the lit windows—and momentarily catharsized tree—it is difficult to say that we know something which the Old Man does not. There must, then, be some understanding in the Old Man that he too is caught in the repetition, although the audience may have enough clues into the power of the repeating dream to draw outsiders into its cycle from the behavior of the Boy. His exclamation that he has murdered twice for nothing is not conclusive. What does demonstrate his awareness of his condition is the careful plan he carries out to free *himself* from the dream, a plan revealed by the line, "My father and my son on the same jack-knife!"[3]

We have already noted that the Old Man repeats his crime. We must note now that he also repeats it in reverse. His second crime cancels his first. Both murders are of an objective person by a subjective one (father and son by the Old Man); both are by the same killer. In this sense the Old Man is reliving his transgression. But the true repetition—from the point of view of the mother's dream, from the detached view of the audience —would have lain in the Boy's murder of the Old Man: both killers would have been sixteen, both victims disreputable old fathers. The fact that the Old Man would be passive in this repetition—being killed by the Boy— would not make it any less *his* repetition; the mother is,

[3] Reprinted with permission of The Macmillan Company from *Selected Poems and Two Plays of William Butler Yeats,* ed. M. L. Rosenthal, p. 208. Copyright 1934, 1952 by The Macmillan Company. Reprinted also with permission of Mr. M. B. Yeats and Macmillan & Co. Ltd. from *Collected Plays of W. B. Yeats.*

after all, passive within the dream that she controls. This is the only reason I can imagine that Yeats would have made both youths the same age at this critical point: to emphasize the repetition and its reverse. In the second killing, the degraded father kills his sixteen-year-old hostile son with the same knife with which in the first killing, the sixteen-year-old hostile son killed the degraded father. Parricide is avenged by filicide. At the same time, the filicide repeats the parricide. The crimes are mirror-images of each other, hinged by the "same jack-knife." Simple repetition leads to the continuance of the dream: more offspring, more killing, no awareness. Repetition in reverse ought metaphysically to be more effective than suicide, as an *antiperformance* of the crime rather than simple atonement for it. Repetition in reverse must have occurred to the Old Man as the way out of a labyrinth of repetition. The fact that this clever plan did not work should not surprise us, however, for in the Old Man's terms it is still necessary for the dreamer to realize the consequence of his transgression upon himself, and the Old Man has only begun to question the efficacy of his murders by the end of the play.

So if repetition in reverse appears at first to be a clever solution to the trap of repetition, it does not resolve the moral implications of the doom to repetition. The souls in purgatory must come to some awareness. If we do not perceive that the Old Man is in his kind of purgatory too, then we accept the closing words of the play at face value: "Mankind can do no more." The mother must go on until the repetitions teach her, or until God gives peace. The audience really has little to say about that. But in the next repetition who knows whether the Old Man will not begin to understand the consequence of his transgression? Doesn't he begin to by the end of the play? Repetition not only operates in *Purgatory* to link dreamers and to emphasize the eternal in the temporal; but it also resembles the insatiable neurotic drives that cannot be resolved in action, that, as Freud observed in his first experiments with transference, compulsively repeat because they are not understood, because this is the neurotic's way of remembering. And there is hope: repeated in a new context—the "playground" of the transference—repressed material may come to seem less traumatic.[4] For the mother as for the Old Man, it is possible that the *next* repetition will bring them closer to awareness of consequence, to critical distance and self-knowledge. The Old Man's final lines are defensive, protecting him from his awareness of

[4] The Oedipal nature of the Old Man's concerns—father murder, mother love, ruin of the house—certainly alerts us, no doubt unintentionally, to the Freudian nature of this repetition. But if we are meant to remember not the Oedipus complex but *Oedipus Rex*, we must still observe that *Purgatory* participates more in the tradition of the Noh Theatre of Japan—where ghosts often require the aid of the living—than in that of Attic tragedy.

being in his own repeating dream, or drama. Perhaps by the next performance of the play he will have learned more.

Further alternatives: 1) The mother need not be in Purgatory at all. It may be the Old Man re-animating the moment which is the focus of his sexual jealousy and the root cause of his parricide. After all, we are aware of the lit windows only when he is. 2) The mother may have absolutely no detachment, thus repeating rather than remembering, and may be re-animating the dream so the Old Man will truly finish the consequence of her marriage by killing himself. As long as he lives— are we really supposed to consider him "harmless," even sexually? [5]—there is still a live consequence upstage. "Mankind" can do one thing more. 3) The stage, rather than the ruins of the house, is the site of Purgatory. All four characters have been in Purgatory, have repeated the entire action, and continue to repeat it as long as the play is performed. The Boy sees the lit window only when he has become part of the dream, by realizing his role as sixteen-year-old objective potential murderer. The audience sees the lights whenever the Old Man does. So the audience is involved in the dream. Purgatory is contagious; the audience is upstage, the more subjective and repeating element downstage. The entire play is a repetition.

Jean Genet's play *The Blacks* is the sum of its per-

[5] Cf. "The Wild Old Wicked Man."

formances, as this final interpretation suggests *Purgatory* may be. It starts over at the final curtain. The audience is being distracted from a real Black revolution which is going on offstage, by Blacks who are attempting to transcend their clown-actor status by continually reliving-through the performance-module. Part of the movement of the play depends on the audience's awareness that this play, which is intended for a white audience, is performed every night and that the total performance occurs only once and will end with the Blacks' arrival at personal reality. During the performance we see, the Blacks are clowns, attempting to tear off the roles and language imposed on them by white men, attempting to find themselves. The Black revolution occurs backstage; the white audience is in front of the stage. A linear progression is reinforced when the play begins again, *farther away from the audience,* at the end. Helically, the play moves in a circle, but progresses linearly. No performance is the same, by context. The sum of the beginnings again, as we shall see later, constitutes a continuous present. The Blacks are moving toward Black reality, toward their own language and action; distracting a white audience is part of that fight, but working through roles, re-enacting ritual—the murder, the entire play—is an even more important part. Blacks have been given their roles by white society even as a white author has given these actors lines. The Blacks are actors in society and on stage. Every repetition of their exploration of this role brings them, like Yeats's ghosts, closer to release from repetition (actors must act each night; people are free), closer to self-actualization. Yeats's Old Man is not the only figure in modern art to suspect that to repeat his crime and simultaneously its mirror-image represents a way out of compulsive repetition. Kharis, too, was doomed to repetition. The solution to the mummy's problem lay in embracing the reincarnation of his beloved princess; when he touched the original, her face crumbled and the bandages collapsed to the floor of the tomb. Doomed to undeath for attempting to raise the princess from the dead, in possessing her he effects her reincarnation; when the second Ananka is as aged as Kharis, they find death together. It is a second Ananka, as the Boy is a second victim, a repetition of the sin (bringing back the dead, loving the forbidden object) that frees the sinner from his atemporal curse. There is a parallel to this sort of solution in Luis Buñuel's film *The Exterminating Angel* (1962), where a group of aristocratic guests trapped without food or water for three months at the site of a dinner party frees itself when one of the guests realizes that they have worked themselves around (as in a permutational board game) to positions in the room (which they cannot leave) identical to positions they had occupied the night of the party. The guests consciously repeat their actions while in those positions—one plays the same piece at the piano, another compliments her on her performance—but with a difference. If they repeated *exactly* what they had done before (and their imprisonment began with a repeated shot of their entering the house, and continues with two different versions of a toast, emphasizing that they are skirting a trap or time-freeze characterized by permutational repetition), the circle would be completed; the game would continue until they were at these positions again, when presumably they would do the same things *ad infinitum*. What happens is that the gentleman who had complimented the pianist and returned to the company now compliments her and says he thinks they'd better be going home. The guests put on their wraps and leave. Their action consists in doing the opposite of what they had done before, but in what looks very like a recreation of the original scene: repetition in reverse, breaking a spell: a succession of slightly changed instants constituting the movement of time. Buñuel has his joke at the end, however, where the same group is trapped in a church with the congregation that has gathered to thank God for the partygoers' deliverance. There is an expanding structure of repetitions in this film, which gives the definite impression of being able to transcend its medium. Every time I have seen this film, the audience gets nervous as it tries to leave.

Hightower too, near the end of *Light in August*, places his faith in a variant of repetition in reverse:

"So it's no wonder," he thinks, "that I skipped a generation. It's no wonder that I had no father and that I had already died one night twenty years before I saw light. And that my only salvation must be to return to the place to die where my life had already ceased before it began." [6]

He is a doom-ghost returning to a familiar spot, seeking *salvation* in dying at the place where he had been robbed of a life in time.

The repetitions in *Purgatory* lock together the past and the present, the immaterial and the material. They are or show the eternal in the temporal. The ghosts and the living and the half-ghosts repeat all together, and their synchronous cycles enlarge a warp between time and not-time until the audience itself is trapped. It is what is repeated that is part of eternity (the dream's actions, the dream). Repetition here is an agency for the transcendence of time—or put another way, a way out of time-freeze *into* time, as it is in *The Exterminating Angel* and *Light in August,* out of the subjective and into the objective, as in *The Blacks*—as it leads the living characters into a dream of the dead. Repetition is also the objective correlative of sin and purgation, of stopped time and the intense investigation of time: the ultimate trap, and at the same time the way out of that trap; the cage and its key; the labyrinth and its solution. The Blacks have been given white man's lines in "an architecture of emptiness and words"; by repeating

[6] William Faulkner, *Light in August* (New York: Random House, 1932); quoted from Modern Library edition, p. 418.

them they can transcend their roles and reach Black reality. We see past the Old Man to the lights in the house, past the illusory dichotomy between upstage and downstage to the purgatorial (cathartic?) link between audience and performance, as the subjective (art) reaches out and dominates the objective (audience)—as the system of repetitions expands past art—as the Exterminating Angel moves from the door of the dining room to the door of the church to the red EXIT sign of the theatre.

From Combray to Marienbad

In Proust's novel, involuntary memory makes a real past instantaneously present. The past experience repeats, and the time that had intervened between the former and present experiences of the event is obliterated. In Beckett's words, "the communicant is for the moment an extratemporal being." [7] One who is simply remembering the past is not extratemporal, since the ordinary sort of memory brings back an imperfect, deliberately noticed image of the past, and not the experience itself. When the impression literally repeats, we are in its time. Involuntary memory is a time-warp that not only returns the past to us, but returns us to the past, makes us who we were when we lived in that time.

[7] Samuel Beckett, *Proust* (London: John Calder, 1965), p. 75.

Where our life has been lost, it can reappear, with a vengeance, as in *Purgatory*, or as a gift, as in Proust, but in either case lifting us out of ordinary time. So long as we do not falsify our past with possession and fear and remembering, we can in the instants of its *repetition* live both in the ordinary "now" and in the "then made now"—transcending our life in space by discovering our freedom in time. The metaphor of "building" time is inadequate in this context, for it fails to reckon with these leaps, this apparent *equivalence* of time, this unstructured interpenetration of past and present. In this subjective construct, there are only variations of the present. The "past" can perceptually repeat just as, in melodramatic metaphor, the purgatorial hoofbeats return with no dimunition in force. The repetition annihilates what has come between, as it does for example in Ingmar Bergman's film *Persona* (1966), where the repetition, from opposing viewpoints, of the nurse's accusatory speech leads directly to her merging with her patient. The *time* between repetitions disappears just as the characters who in a sense are repetitions of each other come together. In identity, space, and time, repetition unifies; but it also allows for progress, as in the succession of identical performances of *The Blacks*, or of rebegun instants in the continuous present.

If memory were only involuntary, however, there would be no common verbal language among men. There would be little abstraction, generalization, or practical communication. Words are not phenomena, but their utility often leads us to make language our primary referent. Language insulates us from experience in much the same useful way as our senses *sample* stimuli. Our voluntary memories are in this sense verbal memories: constructs, rather than sensory Gestalts. Without language, all our conscious functions would be limited, according to Kubie, to "the sensory and emotional recall of fragments of past experiences." [8] Such recall is the Proustian miracle, an answer to death, a nonverbal flash to which hundreds of thousand of words are devoted. But could we live this way, without stamping our experiences under words and logical constructs, outside of time?—or is that the sort of confrontation with reality we would prefer (again) to sample: to discover in the capsule or uneven cobblestone the time-sense of cats, the ambiguity of Alice's Dinah?

The characters of Alain Robbe-Grillet have escaped Proust's problem, but they are caught in his solution. The narrator of *Jealousy*, for example, never discriminates between past and present: all time is present. The narrator is obsessed, and certain scenes that have made a strong impression on him, or that he considers hints of his wife's infidelity with their neighbor, recur continually, generating in their repetition a great sense of

[8] Lawrence S. Kubie, *Neurotic Distortion of the Creative Process* (New York: Noonday, 1961), pp. 138–139.

beauty and mystery. By the time one has finished the book, one has the feeling of having read it many times. The narrator has failed to delimit his identity. He does not generalize. He observes only the surfaces of things: the way a comb runs through his wife's hair, the moving shadow of a column that (because spatial) is his index of time, the pattern of the banana trees on his plantation, the uninterpretable actions of others. He does not discriminate between fantasy and reality. The novel, which is written in the first person, never uses first-person pronouns. One infers from the observations that there is an observer, a person to whom the third glass and third chair—and the mind of the novel—belong. Another way of describing this narrator is to say that he observes only the surfaces of things and of time, has no concept of their underlying concreteness, because his ego-structure is "weak." He is marginal to his marriage. He exists on the outskirts of personal relationship; he does not form ideas about himself; he is as passive, as unself-conscious, and as definitively self-centered as the lens of a camera. But it is also possible to describe his ego as absolute. The definitive quality of his viewpoint suggests in its total subjectivity that the narrator is so secure in his being that his unquestionable identity requires no presentation or defense. He is as clear as his experience—a life-unit that has transcended "personality." This narrator, whose jalousie-bounded point of view is congruent with his jealousy (and whose "objectivity" can therefore be seen as a radically pure subjectivity),[9] whose sense of identity is so absolute as to make first-person pronouns unnecessary or inconceivable, and whose life in time is presented entirely in terms of re-experience—this narrator provides the rationale for one of the most beautiful and obsessive frameworks for repetition in modern literature.

In Alain Resnais' film *Last Year at Marienbad* (1961), for which Robbe-Grillet wrote the screenplay, a woman (A) encounters a man (X) who reminds her that "last year at Marienbad" she had promised to go away with him if he still wanted her a year from then. She does not remember ever having seen him. The setting is a baroque hotel in which all the guests are formal (surface-oriented). In the precise gardens there is a statue that has enigmatic meanings for A and X; the ornate corridors of the hotel are filled with moldings and mirrors. X persists. Finally A comes to believe what X is saying. Her own sense of identity is limited to her surface; her time-sense is limited to the present. Someone else's version of the past can replace her own. She finally believes that she remembers meeting X "last year at Marienbad" and leaves her escort (M). X's reality is

[9] See Alain Robbe-Grillet, *For a New Novel*, trans. Richard Howard (New York: Grove Press, Black Cat, 1965), pp. 138–139. Cf. Gertrude Stein's radical subjectivity which she considered objectivity.

left ambiguous in the final line; X says A will be "alone, with me."

The central ambiguity—whether the "lovers" had met and contracted the year before—is ultimately irrelevant; whether the events of which A was ignorant at the beginning of the film actually had occurred does not change the fundamental insight we gather from the imprecision of her memory. Whether what X made her remember was true or false is irrelevant in a world of surfaces, where any image is equally valid, and less important than the fact that this inability to remember is essential to A's totally present-concerned existence. Nevertheless, the problem has a solution. According to Robbe-Grillet:

The universe in which the entire film occurs is, characteristically, that of a perpetual present which makes all recourse to memory impossible. This is a world without a past, a world which is self-sufficient at every moment and which obliterates itself as it proceeds. This man, this woman, begin existing only when they appear on the screen the first time; before that they are nothing; and, once the projection is over, they are again nothing. Their existence lasts only as long as the film lasts. There can be no reality outside the images we see, the words we hear. . . . And when at the end of the film the hero and heroine meet in order to leave together, it is as if the young woman were admitting that there had indeed been something between them last year at Marienbad, but we understand that it was precisely last year during the entire projection, and that we were at Marienbad. This love story we were being told as a thing of the past was in fact actually happening before our eyes, here and now. For of course an *elsewhere* is no more possible than a *formerly*.[10]

This passage will be dealt with more fully in the next chapter. For now it is important to notice that the discussion has led us from a consciousness of past-present-future time—in which memory and repetition with variation serve to emphasize, echo, label, abstract from, falsify, and organize past experience—to a modern consciousness that entirely disowns "the time of the clocks" [11] and the organized sense of self (however inaccurate) that goes with voluntary memory, building time, and a rigid conception of "character."

Freedom from History

Man has always believed that repetition has the power to abolish time. In the examples above, we saw how moments of repetition (the recurring dream, the past recaptured, the perpetual present of *Jealousy*) expressed the breakdown of building time both in the verbal surfaces of their works and in the vivid "memories" of their characters. Mircea Eliade's study of archaic ontology, *The Myth of the Eternal Return,* demonstrates the fundamentality of repetition in primitive religion and

[10] *For a New Novel,* pp. 152–153.   [11] *Ibid.,* p. 139.

gives many examples of man's reliance on the repetition of events and gestures to abolish history, to continually rebegin time.

Just as primitive man sees an object as sacred because it participates in higher reality (possesses manna or is associated with a god's actions), he also finds it necessary for human actions to participate in higher reality if they are to have any lasting value. Actions are able to do this to the extent that they repeat archetypal actions performed "in the beginning of time"; thus the most important ritual repeats the most important archetypal event: the creation of the world. At the cosmogony, activity, matter, and time began; the cosmogonic ritual is considered to occur *at the same time* as the cosmogony. Primitive man learns from the periodic rebirth of the earth in spring that the pain of winter has no permanent effect, that the spring returns each year with its original vigor: that the destructive actions of time, in other words, are not permanent; that the life-force, whose activity is cyclical, remains indestructible by virtue of its continually starting over from the beginning. To say that spring "returns" would be to posit its continuing existence over the winter, like the second coming of a god. Primitive man perceives this reappearance of vegetation as a "beginning again," from scratch as it were. This beginning again has the psychological effect of negating winter. By *beginning the world over again* in his cosmogonic ritual, man abolishes whatever "profane time" has intervened between the two creations and

thus defends himself against the irreversibility of events
—death, history, winter. Similarly, for Proust, whose
great antagonist is profane time, the repetition of earlier
events abolishes the dead intervening time, reuniting
the lost subject with its lost object. The repeated experience takes place at the time of the first experience, and
liberates Marcel from time's destructive action. In their
linking, both the time of the first action and the time of
its repetition participate in a metaphysic that transcends
profane reality and points to a life in time that is greater
than one can imagine. Proust founds a religion of time
whose basic rite is transcendent repetition; in a sophisti-
cated context, he rediscovers the Myth of the Eternal
Return. (A believer in history, Freud turns repetition
to remembering, helping his patient to see the trans-
ference-repeated event in "perspective.")

When Marcel understands the action of involuntary
memory, his long struggle with his will is resolved; he
becomes able to begin his novel; he finds himself. The
immortality that he associates with art he recognizes is
founded in the redemption of time through involuntary
memory.

Repetition makes identical. People who perform identical actions are related by virtue of that action: *the
differences between them are obliterated, just as the
temporal discrepancies between performances of an
identical act are suspended.* The contrast, in *Le Temps
retrouvé*, between the characters destroyed in profane

time (Charlus, for example, or Marcel before his illumination) and the narrator who has discovered sacred time, and for whom the events and images of his lost life have suddenly regained reality, at first suggests a victory over time. But we should notice that while the repetitive power of involuntary memory in one sense releases Marcel from time, it also gives that time its true value, and makes life in profane time the key to life in sacred time, and life in sacred time the life of "giants." "History" is the province of voluntary memory; it is unimportant, except to the extent that it illuminates what must be outside history.

Just as an event in profane time can take on reality by repetition—as the ordinary uneven tile in Venice, since it is the cause of a repetition, participates in a transcendent time-system, and as the performance of a god's act by a man puts that man in a sacred context or lifts his time back to the time when that act was first performed—so a word can take on more than its ordinary force by virtue of its repeating an earlier use of that word, or can allow a work of art to move as the present moves, beginning again and advancing with the continual youth and power of the present. The aesthetics of repetition thus find their archetype in primitive religion, in the universal belief that an act or a word becomes more real through being repeated, not less real (repetitious). My discussion thus turns to Eliade's comment on Ecclesiastes.

Hegel affirmed that in nature things repeat themselves for ever and that there is "nothing new under the sun." All that we have so far demonstrated confirms the existence of a similar conception in the man of archaic societies: for him things repeat themselves for ever and nothing new happens under the sun. But this repetition has a meaning, . . . it alone confers a reality upon events; events repeat themselves because they imitate an archetype—the exemplary event. Furthermore, through this repetition, time is suspended, or at least its virulence is diminished.[12]

Eliade's belief that repetition alone confers reality upon events supports my suspicion that repetition is not only the great unifier, both in art and in nature, in identity and in time, but also that it is that tool, in a more aesthetic context, whose activity can lead to the annihilation of boredom, to the vitality of language, to the increasing intensity of time and image, through its fundamental sympathy with the rhythms of our desires, of our existence.

Love Letters

Proust's novel brings its narrator to the point where he has just begun to transcend profane time. Long before the final volume of that work appeared in print, however, a literature which dealt with what Gertude

[12] Mircea Eliade, *The Myth of the Eternal Return,* trans. Willard Trask (New York: Pantheon, Bollingen, 1954), p. 90.

Stein called "the continuous present" had begun experiments in time and description that, although many of them built from *A la Recherche du temps perdu,* might well have left its narrator baffled. An examination of the assumptions about the operation of time and memory in the 1945 film, *Love Letters,* directed by William Dieterle and written by Ayn Rand, may serve as a transition to the discussion of this literature.

The romanticism of *Love Letters* begins where that of *Cyrano de Bergerac* ends. Roger Morland, an egotistical and carefree young man, meets beautiful Victoria Remington (played by Jennifer Jones) just before going off to war. He is not a good letter writer, and asks his friend Alan Quinton (played by Joseph Cotten) to write his love letters for him. The film opens as Quinton, who has become very involved with this unknown, idealized woman, writes what he insists is his final letter. It reads in part, "I think of you, my dearest, as a distant promise of beauty untouched by the world." While on leave, Morland marries Victoria. Quinton is wounded and discharged. Back in England, Quinton learns that Morland has died in some sort of accident. Obsessed with the image of the girl he has never met, Quinton leaves his own fiancée and goes to live in a cottage left to him by his Aunt Dagmar, which is not far from the address to which he had written Morland's letters: Meadow Farm, Longreach. On the night he leaves London for this proximate solitude, he attends a party where he meets a mysterious girl named Singleton. He gets drunk and talks about Victoria Morland. When all the other guests have left, the hostess (Dilly) tells him that she knows Victoria and will tell him about her if he ever wants her to. Inland, he visits Longreach and finds Meadow Farm deserted. He returns to London, where through his researches in old newspapers he finds that Victoria Morland had been committed to prison after the murder of her husband. He returns to the scene of the party, where he again meets Singleton, who asks him to tell her about Victoria Morland. Dilly returns, sends Singleton out on an errand, and informs Quinton that Victoria Morland is (as we have suspected) Singleton. This girl of many names has none of her own: she was named Victoria Singleton by the orphanage that raised her, and Victoria Remington by strong stern overprotective Beatrice Remington, who adopted her. She had been found a year ago on her knees before the fireplace at Meadow Farm, with blood on her breast, a knife in her hand, and a look of utter innocence and confusion, over the body of Roger Morland, with Beatrice paralyzed in her chair by a stroke. Victoria's loss of memory was total. As Singleton puts it, because she has no past she has no future; she has only the moment.

Quinton courts Singleton; they fall in love. One night they kiss. Singleton says: "You know what's the difference between us? You're unhappy because that can never happen again, and I'm happy because it's happened once." But there are many repetitions in this story, not the least of which is that they kiss again. For Victoria, for whom the present is all there is, any action has a reality totally independent of its ever repeating, or of its coming after some past and before some future. But the burden of the plot is to educate her through repetition into *remembering,* which is felt to impart greater reality to existence. When Quinton asks Singleton to marry him, something upsets her. From some kind of unobjectified dread—which the audience and Quinton realize represents some half-memory of her earlier marriage—she at first rejects him, then asks him to ask her again: not for emphasis, but to start the question over (begin it again). He does, and everything goes smoothly. When they are about to be married, Dilly asks, "But what will it do to her, the repetition of so important an event?" At the altar, Singleton says, "I take thee, Roger . . ." The priest reassures her that all brides are nervous, and she continues, "I take thee, Alan." The second try works, in both cases, updating her to the present. Of course the audience realizes that this is really the second time Victoria is marrying the same man, since in her marriage to Roger Morland, she believed she was marrying the author of the beautiful letters.

Quinton and Victoria often discuss her amnesia. Quinton, who has decided never to tell her about Roger or the murder and who finds her presentness attractive—since it detaches her further from the profane world, gives her more of that quality "a distant promise of beauty untouched by the world"—does not push her. Victoria says, "I love you but I must try to remember. You do want me to remember, don't you?" and he answers, "Of course I want you to remember. But you can't force your way into the past. You must let it come or not, just as it will." As in the scene of their first kiss, Victoria's presentness is sometimes equated with an absence of responsibility, with looseness, a take-it-as-it-comes present-lust which is filmicly exploited as sexy; but she is moving to responsibility, to foundation in the past, to total "character." (In this sense *Love Letters* is the converse of *Marienbad,* where the present-bound woman is pursued by a lover who *insists* on her confrontation with the past, and attempts to heave her into "reality.") Quinton shows Victoria ten gold sovereigns which his Aunt Dagmar had left for the woman he chose to be his wife. Victoria takes five, saying, "I'm only half a person now."

But the past forces *its* way into the present. The postman delivers a letter from Beatrice Remington in which information is promised about Victoria Morland, and Victoria becomes upset. While picking berries for breakfast, she smears the juice on her breast just as she had Roger's blood before; she screams and starts to remember the murder. Where the Freudian subconscious repeats because that is the only way it can remember, here the life around her repeats parts of her past (letters, blood) and pushes her into relivings. Through the repetition of past events, Victoria is forced to remember. (The berry scene is of course suggestive also of Proust's involuntary memory; it is interesting to find these two memory-systems, which in spite of their different orientations both depend on repetition, serving each other in the popularized memory-construct of *Love Letters*—and later of Hitchcock's *Marnie*.)

Victoria writes Quinton "her first letter"; it contains the words, "I think of you, my dearest, as a distant promise of beauty untouched by the world." After the berry incident, she flees to Longreach in the car Quinton had given her for her birthday (or rebirth, or rebeginning), where she finds her old guardian, recovered from her stroke. Beatrice prompts her memory, and Victoria relives the murder, as the film directly presents it, in flashback.

Victoria had fallen in love with the letters, not with Roger. She had spent all her time reading them. Roger resents her ignoring of his present reality in favor of these relics; his temporal as well as sexual jealousies climax one night, while Victoria is rereading the final letter. "You're going to like me as I am," he threatens; "I'm sick of competing with a ghost." He tells her he did not write the letters, and throws them into the fire; Victoria fights him ("My letters!"); he knocks her unconscious; Beatrice rushes to her defense, stabs Roger, and has a stroke. Victoria snatches a charred piece of paper from the fire ("I think of you, my dearest . . ."), sees the body, picks up the knife and does not know what it is, cleans her hands on her breast. Whether she had killed him or not, she assumes the guilt; it was her responsibility, brought on by her living too much in the past. She protects and punishes herself by obliterating that past. Amnesiac, she lives only in the present, where there is no guilt, no responsibility, no identity, *no history*. Before, her present had been inadequate; now it is everything ("I'm happy because it's happened once").

Reliving the experience, Victoria finds out her innocence. Beatrice could not tell the police what had happened; she could not move or speak. She was waiting for Victoria to come to her. As with the proposal and the marriage vow, the repetition has been more successful —and more *present*—than the original event. Where she had gone to Meadow Farm with the intention of finding out from Beatrice all she could about Victoria Morland, with whom she knows Quinton is still in love, so that she can give him up to his true love (because as her memory begins to return so does her consciousness of guilt)—where, that is, she had gone to give Quinton his past, she has found her own. She turns and finds Quinton in the doorway; he recites a few phrases from his letters and they embrace. He has found his past love and his present love, as she has found that her present love is her past love. And their love begins its third phase, begins on the pure Hollywood foundation of innocence with knowledge, of a vital present informed by a vital past. They have found a life in time (not in the continuous present, since they "begin again" *with* memory), through the agency of repetition.

The earlier phase of their marriage, while Victoria was amnesiac and Quinton silent, can be seen as another instance of repetition in reverse. She is marrying for a second time the man she loves, only this time he is in his proper person. He is marrying the reality whose idealization he had long loved. It is the same marriage, with different people—both removed from their earlier idealizations of each other—and in a sense with the same vows ("I take thee, Roger . . .")—Roger and Alan on the same "jack-knife." But one beginning again is not enough; it is only a step to that complete life in time to which the film's value-structure aspires. The past must repeat in the present; this half-marriage must break up, as it virtually has by the time Victoria flees in her stained dress to Meadow Farm, for the match to be begun yet a third time, with everything remembered. Here, each beginning again imparts a further reality to the union, and advances its development, just as repetition in reverse allows an escape from the time warp. The rebegun Victoria, growing at last to the age of her constant lover, must remind us of the rebegun Ananka.

Repetition resurfaces as the active principle in Hollywood's conception of the time warp in Dieterle's 1955

Portrait of Jennie. Here Joseph Cotten returns as an uninspired painter, and Jennifer Jones as a little girl who can control the rate of her progress through time. When Cotten first meets her, she is a little girl living decades earlier than everybody else; she says she will hurry and grow up faster so they can be lovers. At their next meeting she looks older; she is in tears because her parents, circus performers, have been killed. Cotten checks this and finds that the disaster she refers to had occurred many years before. Things go on like this until she is his age and he is nearly the same age he was when they met. Finally their times synchronize, in her death. She tells Cotten to meet her at Land's-End Light in New England; he does some more checking and finds that a terrible tidal wave had struck this lighthouse long ago, and that a woman had died in the storm. Putting two and two together, he warns the town that the tidal wave may repeat, and goes out to save her. The wave does strike, and Jennie is killed; the wave pulls her away from him, and with an awareness of her destiny in time, she seems almost to let go of Cotten's hand voluntarily. The portrait Cotten executes of her is his finest work.

Again Jennifer Jones's time is different from that of Joseph Cotten, but where before she was immobile and he moved normally, in *Portrait of Jennie* she is supernaturally fast while he continues to move in ordinary time. In both cases she is locked in the past until she synchronizes with normal time (the time of the first tidal wave and that of its repetition being in an Eliadean sense simultaneous); in both cases that synchronization marks the end of the film.[13] In both films she is an inspiration to him, and her atemporality is specifically attractive, suggestive of a lover who gives all and is not answerable to ordinary considerations of responsibility. In *Jennie,* even more than in *Love Letters,* Cotten's attempt to move in Jennifer Jones's time *must* fail—not because he doesn't try hard enough, but because the film will not let him. The film's value-structure forces "realism," "the time of the clocks," on the lovers, determines that their love is doomed but attractively romantic, inspiring but "impractical." Jennie can be captured only in art, just as Victoria Singleton Morland must come to terms with the "touch" the world has dealt her if the "promise" of her beauty is ever to cease being "distant." Both films demonstrate the lust of responsible time for freedom, and in both the repetition of an earlier event is climactic, ending or sealing the heroine's temporal dislocation.

It is a commonplace of metaphysical romanticism, as it is of religion, that there is a reality higher than that which we perceive as ordinary. It should now be possible to interrelate the primitive's use of repetition to project

---

[13] Just as the synchronization of building story and continuing refrain marks the end of the traditional ballad, and as the Mummy and Ananka die together.

himself into "the paradise of archetypes" and to deny profane time; Proust's belief that the reliving of forgotten impressions revealed a means of defeating death; the absolute irrelevance of objective time to the characters of Robbe-Grillet; and the untemperable demonic nature of insatiable repeating drives, which have no conception of time, perceived by Faulkner, Yeats, Freud, and currently—with *Portnoy*—by Roth. Clearly repetition is felt to have the power to negate time just as it has the power to punctuate, create, or transfigure time. Its very quality of being *the same thing again* makes us doubt that this thing was ever not here, or that there was any time in which it could have not been here, any time other than this time—which is, after all, the only time which is real. The past is a construction of our imaginations; our memories change with us. The past is as personal an abstraction as our expectations of the future. No work of art can depend on its audience's accurate memory of something that had occurred earlier in that work; if a concept is important or is changing, it must force itself to our attention again. A book is a string of words that we follow from start to finish; it has a consistent and single time scheme. A film is a ribbon of frames that goes properly in only one direction and has only one tense. A painting is instantaneous, no matter how long our experience of it. The motion on Keats's urn is eternal and still. Like Victoria Singleton, as long as we cannot remember what has come before, each moment can have its full potential for us, need not depend for its reality on any earlier moment. If we think about it at all, we must see that this is how we *do* experience the present. Our relations with the past are part of the present or they are irrelevant: a memory is a conscious act occurring in and created by the present, just as the future is a fantasy of the present. If we don't live now, we don't live. By denying this, we deny ourselves the metaphysical possibility of experiencing reality completely: "excuse me please, I think I'll just hide in the past for a while, see you tomorrow." Living in the present is not godless hedonism, as some of the message of Ecclesiastes is interpreted, but direct experience. Victoria's first kiss occurred once; at that moment it filled all the time there was. It cannot be touched by any future falsifications, nor can its reality be at all influenced by any future repetition or absence of repetition. The memory of it, of course, can be falsified completely.

There is a great deal of repetition in the continuous present, but that repetition is not essential in itself to the reality of the event that occurs in the instant and may or may not repeat. In a properly projected film, no frame repeats. If an identical picture does return later in the presentation, it is an entirely new piece of celluloid, and has no effect on the metaphysical position of the earlier frame. (In the case of a length of film joined at its ends into a loop, the identical frame recurs later in time, and so is a different time-space unit received by a later, aged, audience; it is a later instant of projection even if it is the same piece of film, and completely removed from the art-moment of its earlier appearance. But it can have the *effect* of putting the audience back in that first time.) The frame is projected for a fiftieth of a second or less, but in its instant it is all that is on the screen, regardless of how our memories and experiences receive and integrate it. But for the film to remain coherent, for the audience to realize where it is, the images must repeat, with however slight or radical variation, from instant to instant. The entire image must be begun again, from a blank emulsion, on a white screen.

Most of us have been startled by our science teachers' confident assertion that our cells are always dying and replacing themselves, so that every six or eight years we entirely change bodies. We are a new set of cells every time, begun from protoplasmic scratch, yet we maintain identity. Our existence is dependent not on that earlier set of cells, but on the present grouping. We are our own repetitions. By beginning again, we have continued. But this continuance has no effect on the past we have already lived—as our being dead in the future does not affect the fact that we are alive now.

If this repetition accounts for our present reality, as the rebeginning image on the screen continues the motion picture—if, in other words, repetition and reproduction are singlehandedly responsible for the persistence of life—it may be that repetition represents the

key to a higher reality as well, or to a heightened awareness of common reality. The repeated cosmogony, which
for primitive man rebegins the creation and places him
outside profane time, has its poetic variant in the mantra, where the repeated chanting of a religiously signifi-
cant verbal formula charms the mind into a perception
of a reality that is beyond language or material—just as
a phrase in literature can, if it is repeated enough, take
on a presence greater than that of ordinary language, a
power not approached by the poetry of novelty.

4. The Continuous Present

The first time.
When was the first time.
As the first time it was of no importance.
Another time as permanently and another time just
  as permanently.
Come.
Come.
Coming.
Not just as permanently.
              —Gertrude Stein, *Mildred Aldrich Saturday* [1]

Time in Art

The epigraph above is an investigation of the relative permanence of repetitions. The third line asserts that the time something first occurs is unimportant compared to the times of its repetitions, and dismisses the search for "the first time." We are watching a process of thought that occurs in the present tense of its writing; this is a recorded sequence of deliberative instants. In the fourth line Gertrude Stein asserts that something can have as

[1] From *Portraits and Prayers* (New York: Random House, 1934), p. 115.

much strength in its returning as it has in its first appearance; it can present itself "just as permanently." She begins an experiment. "Come" has the same force its second time as it does its first. But the third time it appears as "coming," which as a gerund or participle is less "permanent" than an imperative. Permanence is of course considered not in the sense of duration but in that of stasis, of insistence—how permanent it is in its instant. She concludes that in a phenomenal world it is not inevitable that every recurrence be "just as permanent."

Up to now this book has dealt with aesthetic constructs in which, through "building," permanence persisted or increased. In examining such writers as Beckett and Stein, however, we must consider permanence in the sense of the experiment above. As readers, we are not presumed able to remember an earlier usage of a word or phrase accurately. It is assumed that we will falsify that perception, as it enters our past, either through laziness or through appropriation to our personal context. It is assumed that if we pay complete attention to the words in front of us, we will need not to be thinking about words that existed in the past. What is important in that past will recur when it is important, in the surface of the text. An image does not acquire an increasing permanence, properly measured at the conclusion of the work, but has its own permanence or laxness at the moment of its occurrence only. That forcefulness is measured instantaneously. An image has presence but not duration.

The present opens the whole of temporal space, just as for Wittgenstein a tautology opens the whole of logical space. Like a tautology it obliterates itself in its formulation, and like a tautology it is unanswerable. The present is equal to itself, as a tautology is a repetition. By living and writing in the present, we may come to our full potential and the full potential of art.

Proust learned that time could be repeated, but not remembered. His novel does explain to us our freedom in time, but that novel itself is answerable to the temporal assumptions and limits of profane time. The eternal present occurs in flashes, but is not taken as a principle of composition. Many readers, of course, are glad that it was not; but since part of what is being argued for in this book is a way of writing consistent with the limits of speech in time, let us consider some of the most important works that have taken that strangely atemporal nature of the present as a principle of composition. We may begin by returning to Robbe-Grillet's version of *Marienbad:*

Last Year at Marienbad, because of its title and because, too, of the works previously directed by Alain Resnais [discussed at the end of this chapter], has from the start been interpreted as one of those psychological variations on lost love, on forgetting, on memory. The questions most often asked were: Have this man and this woman really met before? Did they love each other last year at Marienbad? Does the young woman remember and is she only pretending not to recognize the handsome stranger? Or has she really forgotten everything that has happened between them? etc. Matters must be put clearly: such questions have no meaning. The universe in which the entire film occurs is, characteristically, that of a perpetual present which makes all recourse to memory impossible. This is a world without a past, a world which is self-sufficient at every moment and which obliterates itself as it proceeds. This man, this woman, begin existing only when they appear on the screen the first time. . . . The entire story of *Marienbad* happens neither in two years nor in three days, but exactly in one hour and a half. And when at the end of the film the hero and heroine meet in order to leave together, it is as if the young woman were admitting that there had indeed been something between them last year at Marienbad, but we understand that it was precisely last year during the entire projection, and that we were at Marienbad. This love story we were being told as a thing of the past was in fact actually happening before our eyes, here and now. For of course an *elsewhere* is no more possible than a *formerly*.[2]

2 *For a New Novel,* pp. 152–153. The theory of the unities now is seen as superfluous: an attempt to deny the intrinsic time of art. Almost any play or film takes place in one place (stage, screen) in less than twenty-four hours, and appropriates all its content to one context. What plot-time could possibly undermine the art-time?

In the context of a complex film like *Marienbad* this theorizing may seem obscure, but its accuracy can be verified by applying it to any other work of art. The time of a painting is instantaneous, no matter how long a story it tells. A multiple-image work, such as the *Merode Altarpiece* by the Master of Flémalle, or Warhol's *Ethel Scull (Two Times)*, may be perceived at once, much in the manner of a split-screen motion picture, or it may be followed from image to image. But all the images exist in the same time-format, which is that of the canvas or wood on which they appear.[3] The juxtaposition of instantaneous scenes makes no postulations as to how long it will take the audience to apprehend those scenes; it makes no distinction between the time of performance of the sheet of paper, and the simultaneous presence of its scenes. What is the time of performance of Trajan's Column?

This point can be made more clear if we consider Masaccio's fresco, *The Tribute Money*,[4] where three stages of a story are presented simultaneously by the method known as "continuous narration." A crowd watches Christ direct Peter to find in the mouth of a fish,

[3] The logical expression of this technique in literature is the split page, where for example William Burroughs offers in "Who Is the Third that Walks beside You?" (*Art and Literature* 2 [1964]) three columns meant to be read simultaneously.

[4] Brancacci Chapel, Sta. Maria del Carmine, Florence, c. 1427. This analysis is indebted to H. W. Janson, *History of Art* (New Jersey: Prentice-Hall, and New York: Harry Abrams; 1962), pp. 166, 323–324.

the money demanded by a tax collector, also facing Christ in this central grouping. At the left edge of the fresco, Peter is shown catching the fish; at the right, he is shown giving the tribute money to the tax collector. Peter appears three times, the tax collector twice, and Christ once. In the central grouping, Peter gestures off to the right and the collector to the left, thus directing us around in the story. The three actions take place in a unified landscape, and whatever the time we assume has elapsed for Peter and the tax collector between the scenes in "reality," as far as the work is concerned all three events are equally present. There may in reality have been only one Peter who could be in only one place at one time; but in a work of art, where one is dealing with an *image* of Peter, there is no reason many images may not be presented simultaneously.

In art forms that unfold as they progress in time— literature, music, film, sequential graphics—this simultaneity must be approximated by beginning again. If *The Tribute Money* were a triptych, for example, the mountain before which the three events take place would have to be painted three times instead of once. But whether a work begins again, or is able to exploit the comprehensibility and grace of continuous narration, that work's manifest tense is present, whatever the medium. No matter how long a film is, every frame at the instant of its projection portrays the present—a flashback may be supposed to be occurring in the "then" of the story, but it is on the "now" of the screen, just as it was in the "now" of Proust's mind—and any written word rests on the page, or is read, in its present tense.

Although writing does have words like "then" and "before," these must be considered part of the *content* of the work in which they appear. They are *formally, technically* no more representative of the passage of time than a swirling fuzzy Hollywood flashback-signal. However one rereads, pauses, or skips over this line of words, it has its own time-determination, which cannot be altered by the context into which the reader places it or by the conditions of its reception. Like a moment, it has occurred in its own present and cannot be touched by any future presents. Time is one of the *subjects* of literature, as it is the *subject* of a time-pinpointing word like "before." When Robbe-Grillet omits these words, he does not alter the formal time-sense of his work, but makes it suddenly clear that that undifferentiated present, that natural time-sense of literature and film, is precisely what he is concerned with.

There is some disagreement about what this natural time-sense ought to be called. For Robbe-Grillet, it is a "perpetual present"; [5] for Beckett, an "instantaneous present"; [6] for Eliade, a "continual, atemporal present"; [7]

[5] *For a New Novel,* p. 152.

[6] Richard Coe, *Samuel Beckett* (New York: Grove Press, Black Cat, 1970), p. 17. My discussion of Beckett is indebted to this work throughout.

[7] *The Myth of the Eternal Return,* p. 86.

and for Stein, a "continuous present." [8] The differences
of approach that these terms infer will, I hope, become
clear in the course of this chapter.

I asked earlier whether writing the same work over
and over in different guises was not a sign of neurotic
domination of the creative process. Walter Slatoff's excellent study of Faulkner's *Quest for Failure* and the
following letter from the *Faulkner-Cowley File* may suggest to us that Faulkner's repeating of one essential attempt throughout his works is an instance not of a lack
of artistic control but of "beginning again," in much the
way Beckett's novels begin each other again, continuing
one impossible but necessary philosophic and artistic
(not neurosis-expressive) attempt. In 1944, replying to
Malcolm Cowley's review of *Absalom, Absalom!*, Faulkner wrote:

I am telling the same story over and over, which is myself
and the world. . . . This I think accounts for what people
call the obscurity, the involved formless "style," endless
sentences. I'm trying to say it all in one sentence, between
one Cap and one period. I'm still trying to put it all, if
possible, on one pinhead. I don't know how to do it. All
I know to do is to keep on trying in a new way. I'm in-
clined to think that my material, the South, is not very

[8] "Composition as Explanation," *The Selected Writings of
Gertrude Stein*, ed. Carl van Vechten (New York: Random
House, 1962), p. 518.

important to me. I just happen to know it, and dont have time in one life to learn another one and write at the same time. Though the one I know is probably as good as another, life is a phenomenon but not a novelty . . .[9]

The South was chosen and repeated as a subject because life is not novelty; all subjects lead to the same unchanging subject whose expression, saying "it all," by its impossibility determines failure and by its importance demands trying again. The style is each time the same because it proceeds from the same artistic intention. To fill his works with incest, despair, and frustration, Faulkner need be neither a Freudian nor a Freudian disaster; there are definite artistic reasons for repeatedly investigating the material of the minds of one's characters and for repeatedly straining the bounds of one's ability and medium.

Both Faulkner and Beckett try for inclusive and accurate expression—Faulkner of "it all," and Beckett of the instant, which as we shall see is in its way "all" and impossible to hold.

[9] Malcolm Cowley, *The Faulkner-Cowley File* (New York: Viking Press, 1968), pp. 14–15. One reason Faulkner may have found himself having to begin this attempt again is that "all" cannot be said in words; there is more to reality than the logical. Cf. Benjy's difficulty, from the other side of verbal sophistication: "I was trying to say—" (See p. 175: it *can* all be put on one pinhead, by a mystic, easily, since "the pinhead" and "it all" are one; but it cannot be crammed. Also see note 25, p. 129.)

The continuing nature of reality has passed from a formal characteristic of art to the point where this continuity is art's direct thematic and programmatic concern. If when we remember we falsify, then there must be an art in which the audience does not have to remember what has come earlier in the work, or what is external to the work—one independent from that falsification which has so far been the principal effect of art. Art must falsify its model unless it is its model, unless its occurrence is its subject and appears as it occurs. The aesthetic aim of metatheatre (to create a theatre that is aware of itself as theatre, whose characters know they are actors, as in Genet's *The Blacks*) is frustrated by the necessities of text and performance; for actors are speaking rehearsed lines, and they are not free to reflect spontaneously on their predetermined condition. Even in antitheatre, with its antistage improvisations, the mass cast freakouts give the impression of being planned and paid for. But literature does have the ability to be true to itself (its only "actor" being not the reader but print), to be meta-aesthetically consistent in the teeth of its audience's falsifications. Whether literature can be true to life is another question.

Gertrude Stein

"Gertrude Stein," she wrote of herself, "has always been possessed by the intellectual passion for exactitude in the description of inner and outer reality." [10] Yet her descriptions seem totally unrelated to their objects. We naturally ask, what does the description of Oranges in *Tender Buttons,* "Build is all right," have to do with oranges? [11] Gertrude Stein rejected ordinary speech— which is full of irrelevant associations, connotations, and evocations—in favor of what she considered an accurate, directed, and consistent language, both objective and abstract, whose words and movements would be in her absolute control, and which would not refer obliquely to the associations of old poetry.[12] Stein's manner of recording exactly what she sees—or the movements of her consciousness in relation to its object of attention— in a language that means only what it means *now,* is a discipline of objectivity that her audience has tended to receive as incomprehensibly subjective, if not decadent.

[10] *The Autobiography of Alice B. Toklas,* also cited in Donald Sutherland, *Gertrude Stein: A Biography of Her Work* (New Haven: Yale University Press, 1951), p. 13.

[11] *Selected Writings of Gertrude Stein,* p. 496.

[12] Jorge Luis Borges' story "Pierre Menard, Author of *Don Quixote*" suggests ironically that a cliché can become alive again through repetition that is independent of remembering—that if a modern author wrote *Don Quixote* (using the *identical* words of Cervantes' work) the work would be new and original; the words would have no remembering in them of any earlier usage, as the author would have forgotten Cervantes' book in order to repeat it. Repetition *with* remembering creates history or clichés, from author to author.

For Stein, experience itself "was objective to the point of being indistinguishable from reality." [13]

It is not enough to reinvent language; the act of recording itself must be clear and alive. Gertrude Stein attempted, through simultaneously observing and recording, and by beginning again with each new instant of observing and recording, to make her carefully, consciously chosen individual and nonevocative words record what she actually saw. In her "portraits" particularly, it was important to see each thing, each person, in its or his uniqueness, apart from any resemblance to other things or persons. The success of these observations depended on her being able to see only the present, to write only in the present, to educate her audience to read only in the present.

[13] In attempting to discuss Gertrude Stein, it is important to clarify her distinction between objective and subjective. She was entirely aware that inner and outer reality were not the same thing. We generally assume that inside means subjective and outside means objective, but for Gertrude Stein objective more often meant "accurate." If one's inside can perceive the outside accurately, then the accurate recording of the thinking of that inside should be able to be considered an objective recording of reality. Consciousness and subjectivity are not the same thing; consciousness is the activity and awareness of the mind, while subjectivity more directly implies falsification and contextualization.

The quotation is from Frederick J. Hoffman, *Gertrude Stein* (Minneapolis: University of Minneapolis Press, Pamphlets on American Writers, 1961), p. 13.

The effect of Stein's unfamiliar syntax on our spoken-language-oriented ears is to make us consider each word in the relations which it imposes on the words around it. Every mental observation has its own syntax, or manner of organization. Language changes with its object and subject. As we pay attention to each word, our idealized concentration reveals the exact image these exact words here generate; to what else *can* we relate them but to their simple meaning in their immediate context? Another way of putting this is to say that these words do not "remember" how they have been used before, that their author puts them down as if this were the first time she had ever seen them, as if their present context—since the present is the only existing time, and this syntax defies relation to ordinary syntax or to earlier moments in its own world—were the only context that could ever be important for these words. Each word begins its history in this particular usage.

Her mind free of old associations, literal or otherwise, Stein lets words come together in new ways,[14] as they

[14] If we consider Kubie's distinctions among conscious, preconscious, and unconscious symbolic systems as they affect the creative process—by which a word is tied to a rigid literal association or meaning in the conscious, and to a rigid experiential association in the unconscious, but is free to combine as the changing situation directs or suggests in the preconscious, with creativity defined as the ability to perform new juxtapositions—then we can see the importance of the preconscious in Stein's literary method: although she insisted that her choosing was conscious, and it was. My point is that a free preconscious was

are appropriate and forceful and interesting, in the spontaneous and deliberate act of writing.

There is nothing that anyone creating needs more than
that there is no time sense inside them no past present
or future.[15]

The author must allow her work to take shape in front
of her, with all her concentration. She must move with
of progress of the work, keeping not the past or future
of the work in mind, but only its present; not the past
usages of her words, but her words; not what she remembers the subject looks like, but how it looks. If she
concentrates completely in the moment of writing she
must also concentrate completely in the simultaneous
moment of observation, seeing the object for what it
exactly is, not what it has been compared to or considered. If the grass under the pigeons becomes shorter then
longer then yellow, she can see it and write it. (We begin
to see, perhaps, how Proust's sense of language, his love
of comparison, his sense of past and present and future,
kept his *work* from recapturing the past, and how only

---

vital to the success of her deliberate activity. For "the creative
amalgam of intention and accident," see Richard Bridgman,
Gertrude Stein in Pieces (New York: Oxford, 1971), pp. 240–
242.
[15] Cited in B. L. Reid, *Art by Subtraction: A Dissenting Opin-
ion of Gertrude Stein* (Norman: University of Oklahoma Press,
1958), p. 39.

in nonverbal flashes was his narrator able to put away remembering in the experience of repetition.) She must see in the present, and see the present completely. What is "recollected in tranquility" is falsified.

In the overfamous line "A rose is a rose is a rose . . .", for example, we find what looks very like repetition playing an important part in making a dead word ("rose") real again, removing the word from its "history," and insisting on its existence in advancing time. The difficulty of writing poetry in a "late age," as she explains, is precisely that of giving words life, in the face of all their remembering. Asked by a student at the University of Chicago to explain this line, Gertrude Stein replied:

"Now listen! Can't you see that when the language was new—as it was with Chaucer and Homer—the poet could use the name of a thing and the thing was really there? He could say 'O moon,' 'O sea,' 'O love' and the moon and the sea and love were really there. And can't you see that after hundreds of years had gone by and thousands of poems had been written, he could call on those words and find that they were just wornout literary words? The excitingness of pure being had withdrawn from them; they were just rather stale literary words. Now the poet has to work in the excitingness of pure being; he has to get back that intensity into the language. We all know that it's hard to write poetry in a late age; and we know that you have to put some strangeness, something unexpected, into the structure of the sentence in order to bring back vitality to the noun. Now it's not enough to be bizarre; the strangeness in the sentence structure has to come from the poetic gift, too. That's why it's doubly hard to be a poet in a late age. Now you all have seen hundreds of poems about roses and you know in your bones that the rose is not there. All those songs that sopranos sing as encores about 'I have a garden; oh, what a garden!' Now I don't want to put too much emphasis on that line, because it's just one line in a longer poem. But I notice that you all know it; you make fun of it, but you know it. Now listen! I'm no fool. I know that in daily life we don't go around saying 'is a . . . is a . . . is a . . .' Yes, I'm no fool; but I think that in that line the rose is red for the first time in English poetry for a hundred years." [16]

Nevertheless Stein denied that repetition had anything to do with the success of that line. She insisted in fact that her writing contained no repetitions.[17]

In her verbal portraits Stein was reproached with

[16] Thornton Wilder, "Introduction" to Gertrude Stein, *Four in America* (New Haven: Yale University Press, 1947), pp. v–vi.

[17] For the purposes of my own discussion, in which I have loosely accepted near-repetitions as "repetition," I choose to discuss the aesthetic implications of those near-repetitions that do occur in Stein's work, and to point out how they do contribute to the sense of life that those works show. I am well aware that even hearing an *identical* phrase many times is to hear it in the changing contexts of our reception and the ongoing progress not only of the author's consciousness but also of the work. The discussion of true repetition will have to wait till my final chapter.

being repetitious, and her defense of her method, the lecture "Portraits and Repetition"—informed perhaps even on her part by a confusion between "repetitive" and "repetitious"—makes quite clear her belief that where there is life, there is no repetition. Her use of the term is strict; for her it means identical recurrence with no increase in force, with none of the slight differences in composition that constitute life. Something that is being taught (a piece of knowledge with the excitement of discovery taken out of it) can be repeated in drill; an artwork that simply copies another work can be said to be a repetition; but in her writing there is no repetition.[18] We can see what she means from those portraits.

If we do not pay complete attention to the person before us, we cannot write an accurate portrait of that exact person. To produce these abstract verbalizations of her experience of her subjects, Gertrude Stein trained herself to observe people without caring whom else they were like, and to write with that same concentration, faithful to the integrity of her subject. Each of us is unique, and each of our instants is unique. No matter how many times something happens to us, it is real each time. And each ideal Steinian statement—each new instant of writing synchronized with the subject's fresh movement of consciousness—is unique, and real each time.

[18] "Portraits and Repetition," *Lectures in America* (New York: Random House, 1935), pp. 178–179.

Stein preferred to call her near-repetitions "insistence." In this succession of simultaneously observed and recorded instants she felt progress; remaining in phase with her subject, she believed she accurately experienced and transcribed its identity, its assurance, its "excitingness of pure being."

Existing as a human being, that is being listening and hearing is never repetition. It is not repetition if it is that which you are actually doing because naturally each time the emphasis is different just as the cinema has each time a slightly different thing to make it all be moving.[19]

In comparing the slight differentiation between the successive frames of a motion picture to the differences among her statements and observations—asserting that the differences keep both images moving, just as they constitute the life of the subject—Gertrude Stein makes clear one reason why it is so futile to skim her writing and clarifies her definition of repetition. A motion picture in which each frame was identical would not move. The near-repetition of similar frames, when properly projected, communicates life. If you take a yard of film out of the can and just look at it, you cannot see the movement although you might possibly infer it; the frames look identical. You certainly cannot see how the slight changes act on each other, or feel the movement

[19] *Ibid.*, p. 179.

they produce. Scanning the frames is like skimming Stein; it isn't possible to feel her work without putting yourself in its present. Like each frame of a film, each Steinian statement fills the reader's ideal attention, excluding (by baffling) memory, until the object of her attention is insisted into complex and coherent existence:

Funnily enough the cinema has offered a solution of this thing. By a continuously moving picture of any one there is no memory of any other thing and there is that thing existing . . . I was doing what the cinema was doing, I was making a continuous succession of the statement of what that person was until I had not many things but one thing.[20]

It appears to be the act of saying what something is that divides the perception into instants: observe and record, then begin observing again without any memory of the earlier observation that might obscure or misdirect this observation. In a process not of emphasis but of beginning again and again, she describes what something is, and what it is now, and what it is now.

Just as the primitive kept his world new by yearly returning to the moment of the creation, and by making his life the repetition of archetypal actions gave himself the feeling that time was not irreversibly accumulating,

[20] *Ibid.*, pp. 176–177.

Gertrude Stein's beginnings again keep her writing in its continuous present, keep it alive. She was interested in history, but she resisted "remembering," and felt that "the first time" was "of no importance." While the primitive believed in unbuilding time by returning to Time Zero every year, Gertrude Stein returns to the time of the beginning with each statement, so that there is never any accumulation of building time but an abstract, objective, and jerky continuing.

Implicit in this method of capturing the instant is the assumption that the instant could be looked at hard and precisely. If we hold to the simile of the sequence of motion picture frames, we must see Miss Stein's "film" as like Chris Marker's *La Jetée* (1962), which with one exception is a sequence of tableaux, and there is time to take a good look at each frame—or like the progressing freeze-frames which show one character's memory of the assassination in Costa Gavras' *Z*. Twenty-four frames a second (normal projection speed) is too fast for precise apprehension of each image. Stein's attention slows time: her attention is her time. In reaction to William James's "flow" or "stream" of consciousness, Frederick Hoffman notes,

Miss Stein was much more interested in the fact of an *arrested* consciousness, apparently static and fixed and sacrificing motion or flow to precision. . . . She did not ignore "flow," but found it very difficult to attend to, and dangerous as well, for attention to it ran the risk of losing the integrity and precision of the word-object nexus.[21]

There is progress in Gertrude Stein's narration, but it is slow; and plot, of course ("What Happened"), is not very important. The progress is among the instants, toward complete expression, not, as Reid has put it, toward "the collapse of the artist's attention to his subject." [22] A lecture is over when its audience has experienced its meaning, a portrait when its image is complete, a life when the subject has reached the present or has died. Here are some endings:

Now that is all. ["Composition as Explanation"]

Through to you. [*Four in America*]

And now it is today. [*Everbody's Autobiography*]

And she has and this is it.
                    [*The Autobiography of Alice B. Toklas*]

Gertrude Stein's solution to the problem of the passing present depends on the ability to see each instant distinctly and to record it accurately. Beckett's insis-

[21] Frederick J. Hoffman, *Gertrude Stein*, pp. 12–13. Cf. Heisenberg, Principle of Indeterminacy: choose between the particle and its movement.

[22] B. L. Reid, *Art by Subtraction*, p. 109.

tence on the artist's world as one of failure, of art as a falsifier, and of the present as instantaneous, puts him on the other side of this question. His characters and his art are unable to catch up with time; the Unnamable talks endlessly and at great speed trying to keep up with the fact of his existence or consciousness; Vladimir and Estragon are moving so slowly, have so slowed their time, that what to them seems overnight is for nature a season (the tree blooms between *Godot*'s Acts One and Two) and for Pozzo and Lucky an age; but even so they are the victims of moving time, unable to reach stasis: the temporal equivalent of that silence aspired to by the Unnamable, the end of time. The narrator of *Texts for Nothing* continues his failing as Gertrude Stein continues her beginning, and with that memory that Proust eulogized and Stein rejected ("No, but one last memory, it may help, help to fail yet again").[23] For Stein, language is capable of capturing reality if it puts away memory in accurate present concentration; for Beckett, "words are the chief ingredient of the art of failure." [24] The principle problem with words, according to Beckett, is that they take time to say: they are slower than reality, whose time is the "instantaneous present." [25] Beckett rejects freeze-frames;

[23] Beckett, *Nouvelles et textes pour rien* (Paris: Minuit, 1955), p. 141. Cited in Richard Coe, *Samuel Beckett*, p. 5.

[24] Cited in Coe, p. 11.

[25] See Coe, p. 17. Of course, if each word has all of the awareness in it that it is ever going to have, the time that the word

for him, the synchronization-point of language and time is silence.

The way a motion picture projector works is to show a still frame, darken the screen by closing the shutter, advance the film to the next frame, reopen the shutter and show the next unmoving frame, close the shutter, and so on. Gertrude Stein's instants of perception—of observing and recording, that is, of listening and talking, or of photographing and projecting—are recorded by a still medium, "arrested consciousness," and projected while instantaneously still. The film-advance pattern is ideally identical in both camera and projector; the film, unexposed, is without remembering, and the instant it sees, it records.

Beckett appears to reject this method as one of *art;* the film is stopping and starting, and when projected

"takes" is instantaneous, or identical with that of the awareness. This is what Stein attempted. Narrative is unsuited to nonlinear language; it does take several words to tell a story, and they therefore "take time"; this is what accounts for the frenzy in Faulkner, the anxiety in Beckett, and the assurance in Stein. Faulkner tried to put "it all" in one sentence, but did not give up narrative—in fact crammed in more narrative than most writers; Beckett never quite gives it up—even the Unnamable manufactures fictions, and Mr. Knott's routines are in themselves a story; but Stein is not interested in "what happened." Another point: Faulkner felt that once he had said it all, he would be finished writing; the Unnamable expects that once he is said, he will be able to be still; but life does not stop at being said: it continues to grow and change; Stein knew that "it all" needs always to be said anew, as it all is always new.

has a version of reality, but the reality in question never started and stopped for the convenience of its recording. It continued. The recording of *that* reality is impossible for literature (or photography), but there is nothing else to try. The very fruitful differences between Stein's and Beckett's solutions, which depend on their different conceptions of consciousness, may be made more clear from three comparisons: between *Watt* and *Melanctha* (both early creations—*Melanctha* from Stein's first published narrative, *Three Lives*, and *Watt* Beckett's second and last novel in English—both written on the brink of the abandonment of old language); between "As a Wife Has a Cow: A Love Story" and *The Unnamable* (both products of matured aesthetics); and between the assumptions of time and movement in Stein's play *Four Saints in Three Acts* and Beckett's *Waiting for Godot*. To start things off, I suggest that the difference between the acts of *Godot* is like that between the frames of a film or the sequential insistences of Stein: with Vladimir and Estragon in the limbo of a motion picture camera shooting at ever longer intervals but mercilessly continuing to advance the film.

Stein and Beckett: Beginning Again

The repetitions in *Watt* are actually permutations. Every possible variation of a statement is given in the hope that one of the formulations may happen to correspond to the truth. Watt (unit of work, or of illumination) is a servant in the household of Mr. Knott (enigma, need, nothing). The household is governed by routine. Even when the actions Watt performs and observes are repetitive and trivial, the fact that they cannot be comprehended by the logic of any language, that reality and action transcend the apprehension of a closed system, makes this activity immense and problematic. The unknowable is unredeemable. The pots in Mr. Knott's household cannot be described by the word "pot." When every possibility of statement in the English language has been exhausted, Watt invents other languages, permutations on the structure of English (inverting words, and letters within the words) as he attempts to narrate his experience to Sam, another inmate of something like an asylum. Sam is the equivalent in Beckett's work of Conrad's Marlow: a compulsive narrator with many of the traits of the anti-hero whose tragedy he relates. Thus Sam appears to understand something of the nature of the household, but is quite as unable as Watt to communicate its mystery; his attempt to tell Watt's story exhausts him, and *Watt* ends on a note of "fatigue and disgust." The riddle of action, of phenomenon, by its unknowability [26] drives

[26] Wittgenstein said "the riddle does not exist"; no formulation within language can touch what is beyond speaking of; the solution to the problem is seen in the vanishing of the problem— but neither Watt nor Sam approaches this insight (although, of course, Beckett does), and each continues the impossible attempt to put the question.

the investigative mind to desperations of language. Mr. Knott's household, demanding and defying explanation, obsesses Watt and Sam much as the demon Sutpen possesses the narrators in *Absalom, Absalom!* when they attempt to describe him, their involvement and frustration and the size of the Sutpen action/myth generating the frenzied intensity of that novel's rhetoric. This permutational strategy has three expressions:

1. Listing every relevant fact or object in an attempt to fence in the phenomenon:

And the poor old lousy old earth, my earth and my father's and my mother's and my father's father's and my mother's mother's and my father's mother's and my mother's father's and my father's mother's father's and my mother's father's mother's and my father's mother's mother's and my mother's father's father's and my father's father's mother's and my mother's mother's father's and my father's father's father's and my mother's mother's mother's and other people's fathers' and mothers' and fathers' fathers' and mothers' mothers' and fathers' mothers' and mothers' fathers' and fathers' mothers' fathers' and mothers' fathers' mothers' and fathers' mothers' mothers' and mothers' fathers' fathers' and fathers' fathers' mothers' and mothers' mothers' fathers' and fathers' fathers' fathers' and mothers' mothers' mothers'. An excrement.[27]

[27] Samuel Beckett, *Watt* (New York: Grove Press, 1959), pp. 46–47. This and quotations on the following pages are reprinted by permission of Grove Press, Inc. All rights reserved. Published by Calder & Boyars, London; reprinted by permission.

Although the words "fathers" and "mothers" repeat, there is in the Stein sense no repetition, since each element of the statement is different from the others, and there is a progress toward complete statement—or exhaustion.

2. Listing the logical permutations in an attempt at problem solving:

Twelve possibilities occurred to Watt, in this connexion:
1. Mr Knott was responsible for the arrangement, and knew that he was responsible for the arrangement, and knew that such an arrangement existed, and was content.
2. Mr Knott was not responsible for the arrangement, but knew who was responsible for the arrangement, and knew that such an arrangement existed, and was content. . . .
12. Mr Knott was not responsible for the arrangement, but knew that he was responsible for the arrangement, but did not know that any such arrangement existed, and was content.
Other possibilities occurred to Watt, in this connexion, but he put them aside, and quite out of his mind, as unworthy of serious consideration, for the time being.[28]

Watt's mind is an anguished computer; it adds and is disturbed. He has some intuition, as indicated by his putting aside further permutations (for the time being!), but in general his problem is that he is logic-bound, in a Wittgenstein nightmare, his tool of apprehension

[28] *Ibid.,* pp. 89–90.

the closed logical system of language, which has no direct relation to reality. *Watt* is the extreme working-out, the ultimate parody, of the logic of cause and effect.

3. Carrying logical permutation to the language itself:

So all went well until Watt began to invert, no longer the order of the words in the sentence, but that of the letters in the word. . . .

The following is an example of Watt's manner, at this period:

Ot bro, lap rulb, krad klub. Ot murd, wol fup, wol fup. Ot niks, sorg sam, sorg sam. Ot lems, lats lems, lats lems. Ot gnut, trat stews, trat stews.[29]

But of course, like English, these languages still are closed systems, unable to express the nonverbal or "mystical." From this we infer the limitations of that other great permutational system, Borges' "Library of Babel," which contains all possible combinations of all possible letters; the library must already contain the finished essay "The Library of Babel" that its hero is in the process of writing, and its refutation; but its inconceivable God will be only a God of the Library.

For Beckett, the drive to continue in this hopeless attempt at truth-saying is our only honorable activity

[29] *Ibid.*, p. 165.

within language. Its pain is our proper existential mode. So the attempt begins again, in another list, in another novel. For language to reach truth, and to earn the right to be silent, is the goal of all narrative striving in Beckett's Sisyphean work, and unless language transcends language or time stops, success is impossible.

Language aspires to silence, time to stasis.[30] Denied silence, Beckett exhausts nonintuitive language in frustration at unsayable reality. But Gertrude Stein apparently finds no such trouble. She begins again and again not because each attempt at description or moving-in-phase-with-the-living-object failed and had to fail, but because each attempt, successful and complete in itself, is part of a larger process that depends on this accumulation of instants for its sense of life. The movements of Stein's language and subject are synchronized; but for Beckett, no matter how slowly the time of his works proceeds, it seems always to be juxtaposed with a faster and unknowable time. Perhaps Beckett knows more than Stein; or perhaps he is more afraid of the unprestructured. Both nevertheless begin with prolonged presents, proceed to continuous presents, and in search of a purer present, turn to theatre.

In writing *Three Lives* and particularly the long

[30] Beckett's insight here reminds us of Freud's formulation of the death instinct (the desire of organic matter to return to the inorganic). Watt's smile, for example, has to be "upset" into life, then works itself out so the face can "be at rest again" (*Watt*, p. 27).

story *Melanctha,* Stein developed what she later called a prolonged present, a period of stretched attention in slowed time.[31] This time sense, generated by Stein's devices of "beginning again and again" and "using everything" (see her lecture "Composition as Explanation"), is to some extent discernible in *Watt.* The enigma of Mr. Knott's household is stretched and maintained and examined in what can only be called slowed time, and repetition is the stylistic expression of the continual rebeginning of Watt's investigation, the index of its progress and its urgency. But Watt can remember; he does not start each time from a complete blank (he is, after all, telling Sam what happened in the past).

In the long story of the life of Melanctha Herbert, and particularly of her affair with the doctor Jeff Campbell, repetition has an investigative function within a prolonged situation. We hear, for a great part of the story, an evolving and repeating dialogue between the lovers whose beginning again and again, with reformulations and insistences (and some memory), shows how they are progressing and what they are stuck on and how great their need is to resolve their feelings. They

---

[31] Sutherland, pp. 51–52: "The difference between a prolonged and a continuous present may be defined as this, that a prolonged present assumes a situation or a theme and dwells on it and develops it or keeps it recurring. . . . The continuous present would take each successive moment or passage as a completely new thing." See Stein's lecture, "Composition as Explanation," for "beginning again and again" in *Melanctha.*

are "always saying" nearly the same things to each other. Repetition here is an objective correlative to their emotional states and to the progress of their relationship. (This long dialogue has the same structural role as Watt's immense deliberation over how to give the remains of Mr. Knott's food "to the dog.") As in a repetition compulsion, all of Melanctha's relationships end unhappily, for reasons she does not understand (and as the epigraph informs us, it is neither her fault nor life's).

Jeff and Melanctha experience a difficulty similar to Watt's in that they find it hard to express in their speaking exactly what it is that they are feeling. This problem is complicated by the fact that each of them relates so differently to time and memory. As Melanctha puts it, "I certainly never did see no man like you, Jeff. You always wanting to have it all clear out in words always, what everybody is always feeling. . . . And I don't never any way remember ever anything I been saying to you." [32] Uninterested in memory, Melanctha lives in the present more than the "long thinking" Jeff. Significantly, Jeff is prevented by his time sense and by his concentration from seeing things clearly; he cannot, like Melanctha, "begin again" in that attentive present tense that was for Stein necessary to any real insight:

And Jeff tried to begin again with his thinking, and he could not make it come clear to himself, with all his think-

[32] *Selected Writings of Gertrude Stein,* pp. 407–408.

ing, and he felt everything all thick and heavy, now inside
him, everything that he could not understand right, with
all the hard work he made, with his thinking.[33]

Melanctha's not remembering is the first indication
that Gertrude Stein is moving toward an awareness of
the relation between present-consciousness and "the excitingness of pure being." Melanctha's beginning again,
however, is muddled: there are many things she can
remember and many steps toward self-actualization she
is afraid to take. She remains depressed and unfulfilled:
complex, spontaneous, troubled. It is only when Stein
works through her Proustian interest in resemblance
and the past in her next novel, *The Making of Ameri-
cans,* and emerges with a disciplined attention to the
present alone, that her narrators are freed from the
trouble Melanctha is always finding.

But Beckett never dismisses the problem of memory.
For the characters in *Watt,* beginning again implies beginning with the memory of what has come before, not
beginning again in a new present without memory. The
Unnamable feels the need to recall—or invent—past
identities and a childhood for himself, and Arsene, the
servant who leaves Mr. Knott's household as Watt ar-
rives, observes:

A turd. And if I could begin it all over again, knowing
what I know now, the result would be the same. And if I

---

[33] *Selected Writings of Gertrude Stein,* p. 407.

could begin again a third time, knowing what I would know then, the result would be the same. And if I could begin it all over again a hundred times, knowing each time a little more than the time before, the result would always be the same, and the hundredth life as the first, and the hundred lives as one. A cat's flux.[34]

These lives are like the succession of Steinian statements except that there is remembering in them, which of course defeats the presentness of each life (and the accuracy of each statement). This fantasy is not so much of rebeginning as of extension (a prolonged present). This may be the reason that reincarnation is intuitively attractive only when it is assumed that one will not remember one's previous lives, except perhaps in flashes that give a sense of transcendence. We are content to live it all again "if it be life"; but Arsene's implicit rationalist fear of abandoning memory and knowledge keeps his projected lives from taking on "the excitingness of pure being." His eternal life of increasing knowledge is as limited as Watt's intense and endless investigation, and from the same bias.

The Unnamable starts his new life almost without memory or knowledge, and so is ahead of Arsene on the road to successful existence in the continuous present, although what he is seeking is an end to that present. He soon begins to reconstruct a past for himself—

[34] *Watt*, p. 47.

Beckett's gesture of a plot for the novel. But the novel's true plot is the progress of his consciousness—the ultimate plot in much of Stein's writing too—whose fundamental activity is that of "going on." Begun again, he is forced to continue. He is aware of the distance between language and reality ("call that going, call that on"),[35] he cannot speak and must speak,[36] and in the strict sense, has nothing to speak about; he is unable to measure time [37] or to exist "elsewhere." [38] He exists in one continuing time where it is always present —the time of consciousness—and in one nonplace. He does nothing and is nowhere; he is manifested only in language, yet is unnamable. His sentences characteristically are full of interpolations; he cannot deliberate and then utter in order. His language moves as fast as (in fact is) his consciousness, running and staying in the same place like Alice.[39] He is the archetypal Beckett character, whose images in the earlier novels are Molloy, Murphy, Malone . . . and who is angered at having been roused from unconsciousness into speech

[35] *The Unnamable,* in *Three Novels by Samuel Beckett* (New York: Grove Press, Black Cat, 1965), p. 291. Translated from the French by the author. Copyright © 1958 by Grove Press, Inc. This and quotations on the following pages are reprinted by permission of Grove Press, Inc. Published by Calder & Boyars, London; reprinted by permission.

[36] *Ibid.,* p. 301.   [37] *Ibid.,* p. 299.

[38] *Ibid.,* p. 297. Cf. Robbe-Grillet, *For a New Novel,* p. 153.

[39] See several interesting discussions in the *Alice* books of the problem of beginning again, of identity in the continuous present,

—that is, into another novel. (There is a close analogy here with repetition compulsion: the longing of the roused language for silence.) Beckett has stripped almost all pretensions of plot and character from the act of writing in an attempt to push language to that point where it really confronts the objects of its falsifications, to the protoplasm of fiction. The Unnamable is as anxious as Watt, although not as determinedly logical (whatever thoughts he has are incidental to the act of speaking); in both, however, confrontation with enigma drives them to try to explain, to push languages to their limits, to say the unsayable and be at rest. If we return to Arsene's version of reincarnation, we can see that *The Unnamable* represents a change in Beckett's way of conceiving beginning again. The Unnamable wakes from anonymous unconsciousness to anonymous consciousness, without real memory or the ability to remember, only the ability to keep trying to express his condition accurately, in order that his expression may be completed; Arsene would begin again with all his knowledge from earlier lives. The Unnamable makes up all that he discovers, but even that is hard won. The

---

especially " 'I could tell you my adventures—beginning from this morning,' said Alice a little timidly; 'but it's no use going back to yesterday, because I was a different person then.' " ("The Lobster-Quadrille") Also several anticipations of Beckett in the Mad Tea-Party: the way time was stopped at tea-time by a time referred to as "him" (evening, Godot), and the inhabitants of the treacle-well who drew "everything that begins with an M—"

Unnamable has no conception of an objective "past present or future"; every instant of conscious activity is new. Beckett's sequence of novels with the same archetypal character—but with each attempt at that character a new one—can be compared to a sequence of Steinian statements, each a beginning again, with an occasional Proustian flash from novel to novel, as when the Unnamable "remembers" his other manifestations. And the sequence has reached its near-end, its almost-object, in the archetype of its earlier expressions.

We do not know whether silence is reached, since we do not know whether the end of the last paragraph is the momentary silence which separates paragraphs or the lasting silence, resolution and identity:

. . . all words, there's nothing else, you must go on, that's all I know, they're going to stop, I know that well, I can feel it, they're going to abandon me, it will be the silence, for a moment, a good few moments, or it will be mine, the lasting one, that didn't last, that still lasts, it will be I, you must go on, I can't go on, you must go on, I'll go on, you must say words, as long as there are any, until they find me, until they say me, strange pain, strange sin, you must go on, perhaps it's done already, perhaps they have said me already, perhaps they have carried me to the threshold of my story, before the door that opens on my story, that would surprise me, if it opens, it will be I, it will be the silence, where I am, I don't know, I'll never know, in the silence you don't know, you must go on, I can't go on, I'll go on.[40]

We notice that "they" have dropped out of the final goading; there is no second "you must go on." (We also notice that a close repetition seems an aesthetically successful way of resolving a string of repetitions: "I can't go on, I'll go on.") The goad to beginning the discussion again, in the hope of achieving a dynamic and accurate correspondence between language and reality and an end to pain (life, frustration, impotence), has in *The Unnamable* finally confronted the danger of anonymity, of surrender to the inexpressible and uncontrollable; identity has been renounced, but life has persisted, and the unknowables and unsayables whose knowing and saying is the mission of the existential artist—and which must be dealt with before any "story" can be told or identity affirmed—have been brought infinitesimally closer into range.

Gertrude Stein's story-portrait "Miss Furr and Miss Skeene" is of course not of the complexity or length of *The Unnamable,* but it is a good example of her work in the continuous present. It may profitably be read in conjunction with "As a Wife Has a Cow: A Love Story," which begins by defining its terms (*Unnamable:* "I, say I . . . call that going, call that on"; *As a Wife:* "Nearly all of it to be as a wife has a cow, a love story"),

[40] *The Unnamable,* p. 414 (end of the novel).

proceeds through variations on those terms and on time ("Not and now, now and not, not and now, by and by not and now . . ."), and reaches its resolution in a completeness of statement and realization of story and identity analogous to the Unnamable's silence ("My wife has a cow").

"Miss Furr and Miss Skeene" gradually tells the story of two women who live together for a time and "cultivate their voices," then grow apart. Together, "they were regularly gay," and when Helen Furr is on her own again she lives "regularly" and is gay in telling all the little ways she had learned of being gay. The continuity of her existence, and its expanding happiness, is put in terms of her repeated telling of her knowledge of living:

She told many then the way of being gay, she taught very many then little ways they could use in being gay. She was living very well, she was gay then, she went on living then, she was regular in being gay, she always was living very well and was gay very well and was telling about little ways one could be learning to use in being gay, and later was telling them quite often, telling them again and again.[41]

The gaiety and its discussion continue together with no loss in vitality. This quality of keeping subject, object,

---

[41] *Selected Writings of Gertrude Stein,* p. 568 (end of the story). See Bridgman, pp. 95–96, on the question whether this ending is ironic. My point is the same whether Miss Furr was

and speech in phase in continuing time is what the Unnamable, on Beckett's behalf, is trying to achieve.

The similar movements of "As a Wife Has a Cow" and *The Unnamable* make clear that although Stein is concerned with psychology and Beckett with philosophy, the two writers approach the problems of time and language with similar literary tools: notably repetition in the continuous present. I am not suggesting that Steinese offers a resolution to the problems of existentialism, but it is interesting that their evolving attitudes toward beginning again and memory are so closely related. Beckett's conviction of failure and the need to continue, and Stein's conviction of success, are both addressed in one sense to the difficulty of creating internally consistent writing, writing which in itself *is*. Both are aware that they are trying to do the impossible or at least the very difficult. Beckett's urge to failure has been discussed already; it remains to add that one of Stein's mottoes was "If it can be done why do it." [42]

Theatre and the Continuous Present

Both Beckett and Stein turned to theatre for its flawless present tense. Stein's plays, which aim at an

---

actually gay or was anxious to appear gay: the being and the telling are synchronized.

[42] *Lectures in America*, p. 157.

abstract and straightforward simplicity, nevertheless require some introduction. They are conceived as "movement in a space or in a landscape"; [43] they are what can be seen by looking at it. Free from plot, they are nearly free from causality; they consist mostly of "playful" juxtapositions, made up of movement rather than consequential action. A situation is presented, in relation only to itself; it exists rather than informs. Characters do not always have names, and even when they do we cannot describe their identities with the limited index of "personality"; sometimes there are just numbers with styles—but they have definite being. The idea in her first play, *What Happened,* was "without telling what happened . . . to make a play the essence of what happened." [44] There is a great vitality in Stein's plays; we become interested in the action not because we are being built to a climax, or because we are watching characters clash with themselves and their environment, but because the characters and their environments, as a consistent landscape, are moving in phase: in short, appear not to move in any direction, but project the energy of motion:

But the strange thing about the realization of existence is that like a train moving there is no real realization of it

[43] Sutherland, *Gertrude Stein: A Biography of Her Work,* p. 125.
[44] Gertrude Stein, *Lectures in America,* p. 119.

moving if it does not move against something . . . if the movement, that is any movement, is lively enough, perhaps it is possible to know that it is moving even if it is not moving against anything.[45]

Four Saints in Three Acts is static in the sense that it is not moving in relation to anything else; but everything in the play has its own energy: the energy of a living work. Its author said, "anything that was not a story could be a play," [46] because stories involve suspention of attention from what is going on in the theatrical present. What else is a play but something going on and being looked at—a stage landscape in juxtaposition with an audience landscape? This book is something going on on a page; if it were a poem it might take on the dynamic spatial arrangement characteristic of actors on a stage. You reading this are outside but attentive, and in our juxtaposition there is an energy independent of your reasons for reading this or my reasons for writing it. How you came to be facing this page or my words to be on it are stories, of less interest than the dynamics of our current relationship, which is one of presence. If I were to abandon logic in this work, there would be little for me to do but continually to confront you with my presence and its process. Soon I would turn to poetry or calligraphy in an attempt to

[45] *Ibid.*, p. 165.
[46] *Gertrude Stein: A Biography of Her Work*, p. 113.

dramatize our relationship, to give it spatial energy. To insist on the present quality of our time together, I would at some point turn to theatre.

Theatre is a good vehicle for the art of the continuous present for two reasons: a play occurs before the audience in the present and keeps moving, and its materials are presented with reference only to themselves and are therefore dependent not on causality but on juxtaposition and repetition. Energetic occupation of space: that seems to me the nature of landscape in theatre. Ideas can be spatially juxtaposed, can be emphatic about their existence, much as a mountain and valley spatially *are* and insist. Such a theatre is not limited to the dance; Stein's theatre certainly demonstrates that anything from an abstract version of the life of Susan B. Anthony, to counting, can take on spatial energy in a continuing time. Stories are distractions; situation is truth.

Gertrude Stein presents motions that stay in place— as good a definition as I can find of the quality of excitement and stasis (waiting) in *Godot*. Both *Godot* and *Four Saints* are plays of landscape, yet both progress to what feel like endings. Both are static yet develop, and in both, as Sutherland says, "the heart of the matter is constantly there." [47]

[47] Conventional dramatic structure generally keeps the audience catching up with it, rather than allowing stage and audience time to move together. In the theatre of repetition, these

The heart of the matter in *Waiting for Godot* is, simply, waiting. Vladimir and Estragon meet on a country road in the evening, wait for Godot, encounter Pozzo and Lucky, and are told by a boy that Godot will be there tomorrow. That is the plot of each of the two acts. The two tramps move infinitesimally closer to Godot in the course of their play; the action is not over for them, but it feels proper that it should be for us. The ending of the second act is very much like that of the first, but some forward movement has occurred (enough for us to guess how a third act would move) and has been perceived through the discrepancies between the near-repetitions of the two acts.

---

times attempt continually to be in phase, without remembering, in the present. As Donald Sutherland puts it, "Gertrude Stein was right enough when she pointed out that the emotion of an ordinary stage climax is essentially relief, that is, a relief over having at last caught up with the heart of the matter. She meant instead to create something in which the heart of the matter would be constantly there" (*Gertrude Stein: A Biography of Her Work*, p. 115). The clearest example of this kind of play is the mystery drama that is solved at its end. Such plays are of course primarily concerned with "what happened." In a theatre that cared more about the essence of what happened, a mystery might look very like *In Circles* or *Waiting for Godot*. The solution would be always on stage but never "solved in the action." The mystery and its solution would be identical, and always present; one would always be caught up, and would ideally feel a complete movement in the mystery. A mystery novel in the continuous present might look more like Robbe-Grillet's *Jealousy* than his *Erasers*.

Vladimir and Estragon's waiting is made bearable by the impermanence of their memories; they have always been here; they cannot really remember the first act by the time they are in the second; they have to move in the present. Vladimir remembers the Boy who does not remember him, but he does not make enough out of this to be said to become entirely aware of the repetition. It is generally true of repetition that if one is involved with what he is repeating, if for him and his audience the word or action has the life and meaning of appropriateness and discovery, recurrence will not be felt as repetitious. It may be felt as "insistence" or simply as energy, but it will not be dead. We can repeat a line fifteen times in a short poem if we believe in it; we can read that poem if we do not rush over the repetitions with mental ditto marks; we can move with the vitality of each identical sunrise; we can make love to the same person if we are in love. It is not important that we have done or felt or said these things before; memory only displaces or undermines our objective experience of the present. *In the continuous present there is no consciousness of repetition.*

The two acts in *Godot,* which change but repeat, and in which there is only the most imprecise kind of remembering, thus approach the nature of successive statements in Steinese (cf. *Four Saints'* stage direction, "Repeat First Act"). They are the fixed-while-exposed frames of the motion picture, between which there is darkness. The time of the tree speeds past the time of the tramps, as the stasis-and-advance-with-slight-change art-time of motion picture film cannot approach the always there and always changing objective reality before the lens. The time of the tree is smooth and fast, that of the acts jerky. The speed of the tramps appears slower the more it increases (approaching the speed of light? the time of the tree?). Their waiting begins again with each long day.

Identity is a matter not of $x = 1$ or $x = 2$, but of $x = x$; the self is not a name. Stopping the search for self at "personality" is like being electricity and deciding that one is whatever has been plugged in—a toaster, for instance. We change as we move in time; moving in relation to nothing but ourselves, we grow and have life, and are life. We are unnamable, not simply M— after M—. Time counts one, one, one. Units succeed each other but in the continuous present do not build; and even this concept of units is true only in art: time does not count at all.

Stein's saints "have to be to see," and "to see to say." [48] The Unnamable must say until he is. Because the saints *are*, because they can listen and talk at the same time, without identity-anxiety, their speech can present reality and move at its speed. Beckett's characters have not definitively found their selves; they wait

[48] Gertrude Stein, *Last Operas and Plays,* p. 480 (from the finale of *Four Saints*).

for time actually to stop so they can see it; the tree would have to be as fixed as their frame (as in *Endgame,* where nature *has* almost stopped): a still photograph of a still object, not a motion picture (depending on a trick, persistence of vision) of a continuous reality. His speakers are only approaching the identity—entirely without memory, entirely in being and being in the present—that will free them from the need to talk: in which experience, language, and time will synchronize in silence.

Art and Experience

The question is whether experience can be caught in time—whether any act of recording can approach the act of living. Words and frames occur singly, and accumulate into statements or movements. It is in their nature to divide experience and to present pieces of experience in sequence, trusting the act of apprehension to restore continuity. They make it necessary for us, and thus instruct us, to apprehend the present, a perfect continuum, as a series of instants. It is this act of division which distinguishes art from experience. Pure continuum remains inexpressible; while we are aware of its nature (when, for example, we experience the enormity of actual *love,* and no italicizing or adjectiving or framing or insisting will begin to express or image that transcendence which is falsified even by being called "feeling") the act of dividing and arranging and killing into the communicable is laughable to us, and horrible. There is no *need* to say such things: we say them in living, becoming and answering such experience *with experience,* rejecting all art-methods, rejecting what always is false.

And the truth then is seen as greater. It is not simply the illuminated moment that cannot be put into words: it is all experience. Reality, because it is continuous— always the real, always present, always what life is and the way life has of moving through itself, so that time and reality are one, and one with life, as existence and experience are one—is necessarily and always outside the verbal, or divisible. It is typical of our need to habituate ourselves to experience that we are aware of this intense continuity only in extraordinary moments, gasping and laughing at ourselves at the absurdity of "I love you," later remembering—such is voluntary memory—only the terrible words. But *all* of reality is unnamable. There is really not so much difference between Watt's "pot" and "love"—or "Incarnation," or "I." All of our words are in quotes.

Thus when Stein takes the present by instants she is working comfortably within the limits of art, perceiving, as the director Jean-Luc Godard put it, the "truth" twenty-four times a second; or, as Stein said, "every time it is so it is so." [49] (Of course Godard, a

[49] Gertrude Stein, *The Geographical History of America,* p. 85.

sometime believer in art, did not put truth in quotes.)
It is in the supreme distrust of Beckett, and in the
wrenching honesty of Agee's *Let Us Now Praise Famous Men*, that we find art responsibly, desperately
hating itself, pulling for the real, for the intense expression of continuity. And we know they must fail,
that the acts of *Godot* are frames, and art a camera, for
which reality will not stop: that Agee's raging experience of humanity will be picked up, his people's *living*
will be picked up "as casually as if it were a book." [50]
And of course he has asked for this, by making a book.

The instant-method does what art does, frame after
frame. Dividing the present is a falsification, and near-
repetition perfects this method, but does not undo the
damage. The continuous present, to be experienced,
must not be split. If we must suffer the fall into language, we must still try to undo the divisions of
verbiage, and the false connections of syntax, in a
nearly preverbal discipline of true, not near, repetition. We will deal first with the attempt at literal
repetition in art, and then drive if we can past art, past
the aesthetics of near-repetition, to the experience of
the timeless, the unquestionably real, the undifferentiable: where as unnamables we will not feel that we
must speak until we are said: where, like Antoine
Doinel in Truffaut's *Stolen Kisses*, we can say the mys-

[50] James Agee and Walker Evans, *Let Us Now Praise Famous Men* (Boston: Houghton Mifflin, 1960), p. 13.

tery of our name into the mirror so many times that the name becomes impenetrable and we are gladly rid of it.

Alain Resnais

Both emphasis and falsification depend on remembering. Repetition with remembering emphasizes up to a point; then it creates its own monsters, and finally deadens them into routine. But repetition without remembering can renew.

By this reasoning, even a film loop would not be boring so long as we did not, as an audience, approach it with remembering. Nevertheless, such a loop would not be a good artwork about repetition, since it could not manifest that developing consciousness which we have seen is essential to the vitality of work in the continuous present. There would have to be an active mind, in the work, for whom each repetition was a new experience. The audience, attentive to the development of the hero's consciousness as manifested in the work's repetitions, would soon comprehend, if not experience for itself, the nature of repetition without remembering.

Alain Resnais, the French director whose central theme seems to be the interrelations of repetition, remembering, and love, has at last given us such a film—or half of such a film—in which scenes repeat without variation and yet manifest advancing consciousness. Before discussing *Je t'aime, je t'aime* (1968), let me review Resnais' earlier work.

The intrusion of something past on something present is Resnais' virtual signature. *Nuit et brouillard* (1955), for example, intercuts a concentration camp's present (overgrown, peaceful, in color) with its past (horrible, black and white). *Marienbad* may be its own "last year." *Muriel, ou le temps d'un retour* (1963) counterpoints a young man's obsession with an atrocity in which he had participated during the Algerian war, with his stepmother's attempt to rebegin an old love affair under a load of false memories. The young man's memory is goaded by an 8mm film of happy soldiers taken in Algeria; the stepmother has a bad memory (like Beckett's Proust), and her lover falsifies the past to such an extent that they both become aware that their nostalgia is for a nonexistent past. The stepmother puts off a constant present lover in her obsession with her first; the young man, all the time compulsively documenting the present, speaks of his girl friend, Marie-Do, as if she were Muriel, the subject of the atrocity. When the falseness of her own memories is exposed, the stepmother becomes involved in the story of Muriel (Marie-Do). This film deals with the past exclusively in terms of the present, that is of its falsifications. Instant succeeds instant; there are no dissolves or fades, only straight cuts. The present is never mixed with any other time.

In *Hiroshima mon amour* (1959) a French actress has a short affair with a Japanese architect. The twitching of the architect's hand in sleep reminds her of the reflexive twitching of the dead hand of her first lover, a German soldier. In both affairs she loves someone from a country France had fought in the war; she has in fact come to Hiroshima to make an antiwar film, starting herself back to the time of her earlier affair. This affair is no more successful than the first, although we can see that it might have represented a repetition in reverse (Germany victimized France, France as an Allied power indirectly destroyed Hiroshima; the actress has come to Hiroshima out of an involvement with its past, while the architect is operating in its present with an eye to its future).

Je t'aime, je t'aime deals not with memory but with repetition. Claude Ridder survives an attempted suicide and is persuaded by a group of scientists to test their subjective time machine. He and a mouse will be sent, for one minute, one year back into their own pasts; they will experience that moment and return to the present. Claude had tried to kill himself out of the guilt he feels at having murdered his mistress, Catrine; compulsively involved with his past, and uninterested in living in the present, he lies next to the mouse in a womblike structure and is reborn into his past. The moment to which he is returned is shown directly on the screen: no fuzz, no framing, *no dissolves*. He is swimming underwater for the whole minute. That moment occurs in the present tense of the film, just as it repeats for Claude, who relives it with no temporal distance, no "remembering." (Resnais' manner of cutting among times without dissolves or fades makes an important point: one does violence to realism by any kind of cutting, moving from one shot to another. *Any straight cut is a time-leap.* The year-leap in *Je t'aime* is as cinematically consistent as the jump-cut in *Muriel* from a full serving dish to the dish and its leavings when the meal is finished, or from over Cary Grant's shoulder as he talks with Joan Fontaine to over Joan Fontaine's shoulder as she talks with Cary Grant.) Claude disappears from the water, reappears in the time machine. Then he disappears again. He swims toward the camera again. He is caught in that moment. The identical shot repeats; we infer that his involvement with the past is keeping him from returning to the present (or, since the mouse is having the same trouble, that the machine doesn't quite work). The choice of an underwater moment is perfect: the audience feels out of breath, demands that Claude get out of the water, into that past, for oxygen. The next shot shows Claude wading in, backward—a physical gesture that perfectly conveys the multiple tensions of his time-choice, not a reversed film, nor a variation in what had occurred. He swims toward the camera. He is back in the time-womb. He is on the beach with Catrine.

From there the film presents scattered past instants, all present to the time-traveler; he is not looking over anybody's shoulder. Repetition is far better than nostalgia and guilt, or remembering. The sequence of scenes becomes rhythmic, as certain of the repetitions (notably those of wading and of swimming) repeat. He relives enough of the affair to let the audience know why he tried to kill himself. The resolution of the film is reached when he relives the moment of his suicide. He reappears in the scientists' present, outside the time machine, dying of his wound. We do not know whether he dies this time.

Here the repetition in reverse (of the suicide) is done not through memory, as in *Hiroshima,* but in the actual time of its earlier occurrence and simultaneously at a later point in the film and in Claude's subjective experience.[51] The last thing we are shown is film-time actually stopping. The mouse had gone on a temporal juggernaut like Claude's (at one point their pasts intersect: Claude and Catrine wonder what a white mouse is doing on the beach); with Claude returned to the present, the mouse is seen in its bell jar, sniffing upward for air, in a freeze frame.

Although the movement of the plot is melodramatic (the scientists' attempts to save Claude are pathetic neo-Hitchcock, and ruin half the film), *Je t'aime, je t'aime*

[51] So these are also Eliadean repetitions. Cf. Marker's brilliant film of "a time twice-lived," *La Jetée.*

is a genuine exploration of the continuous present and of the implications of montage. The nature of that present is put in terms of repetition: all instants in time, all shots in film, are of equal value, equal permanence. A shot recurring on the screen *repeats*, with no framing, in the present—just as Claude relives his past in his present. (And Claude moves among places and times without the time machine's moving, just as remote places and times are juxtaposed on the fixed theatre screen.) There is progress in this repetition, as in *Purgatory* it is hoped there is progress. Of course this film is exactly the record of a purgatory, where by repeating one's sin one may come to an understanding of it, may bring it into one's present (as Claude brings his wound), may bring one's subjective time into phase with "outside" time. Sin stops time,[52] just as any really important action holds one's attention; that sin must be worked through or purged for us to say, "The time is free!" From its double title forward, *Je t'aime, je t'aime* is a compact expression of the difference between remembering and repetition, as it is a demonstration of the way art continues in its present tense regardless of the story-tense of its scenes or shots or sentences. Every shot is equally present; there are no framing dissolves —cinematic equivalent of "then," "later," "before"— *anywhere* in the film. Every instant is new. Even when

[52] Cf. *The Unnamable,* p. 414: "strange pain, strange sin, you must go on . . ."

a shot is repeated many times (he swims toward the camera), the film-time is advancing, continuing its image, and the audience is feeling each breath-held sixty seconds—a very long time in film—with real intensity, real need for oxygen, at every repetition. That shot is not remembered; it is *here*.

"I'm sure I'll take *you* with pleasure!" the Queen said. "Two-pence a week, and jam every other day."

Alice couldn't help laughing, as she said "I don't want you to hire *me*—and I don't care for jam."

"It's very good jam," said the Queen.

"Well, I don't want any *to-day*, at any rate."

"You couldn't have it if you *did* want it," the Queen said. "The rule is, jam to-morrow and jam yesterday—but never jam *to-day*."

"It *must* come sometimes to 'jam to-day.'" Alice objected.

"No, it can't," said the Queen. "It's jam every *other* day: to-day isn't any *other* day, you know."

"I don't understand you," said Alice. "It's dreadfully confusing."

"That's the effect of living backwards," the Queen said kindly: "it always makes one a little giddy at first—"

"Living backwards!" Alice repeated in great astonishment. "I never heard of such a thing!"

"—but there's one great advantage in it, that one's memory works both ways."

"I'm sure *mine* only works one way," Alice remarked. "I can't remember things before they happen."

"It's a poor sort of memory that only works backwards," the Queen remarked.

> —Lewis Carroll, *Through the Looking-Glass,*
> "Wool and Water."

5. Jam Today

> When in a mountainous region one hears the wind day in
> and day out execute firmly and unchangingly the same
> theme, one perhaps is tempted for an instant to ignore
> the imperfection of the analogy and to rejoice in this
> symbol of the consistency and assurance of human freedom.
> —Søren Kierkegaard, *Repetition*

Beyond Logic: Repetition as Syntax

So far I have discussed repetition as if it were some
unstable artistic compound: handle it carelessly and it
will kill both you and your subject, handle it in full
awareness of its properties and with a genius for its
use and it will serve you well. My aesthetics have con-
sisted in attempting to clarify these properties and to
define care. But aesthetics is often a discipline more of
philosophy than of art. The continuous present is not
an invention of philosophy, but the time-conviction of
a student of consciousness. Even so it has led us to the
problem of time and the problem of transcending limits:
problems with which philosophy and religion have
perhaps better equipped us to deal directly than have

psychology, poetry, and film. If I have built up a theory of repetition in and out of time, in and out of art, the consistency of that theory is owing not to some three-thousand-year artistic conspiracy, but to what I am attempting to define as the innate character of repetition, a poetic and thematic nature that has made itself clear to hundreds of artists independent of any latter-day philosophizing. I feel it necessary here to attempt to touch directly this nature, this fundamental tendency that I believe is to timelessness, and I must turn to three philosophical/religious texts, hoping that they may make my concluding argument clear: Wittgenstein's *Tractatus*, the Hindu Upanishads, and Kierkegaard's *Repetition*.

Language has definite limits; there are some things of which it cannot speak. Because language is logical, it cannot describe the illogical any more than we can, strictly speaking, think the illogical.[1] Just as, to the religious, there is an incomprehensible force outside the world, to Wittgenstein and Beckett there are realities outside logic, events neither caused nor causes, awarenesses that cannot be verbalized.

The outgoing servant Arsene attempts to explain Mr. Knott's household to Watt, Watt to explain the household to himself and to Sam, and Sam (with his novel)

[1] "Thought can never be of anything illogical. . . . It is as impossible to represent in language anything that 'contradicts logic' as it is in geometry to represent by its co-ordinates a figure that contradicts the laws of space, or to give the co-ordinates of a point that does not exist." Wittgenstein, *Tractatus*, 3.03, 3.032.

to tell it all to the reader. Sam is prevented by "fatigue and disgust" from completing his record; Arsene speaks in the moment of giving up; and Watt, as a logical positivist, is defeated by definition. None of the three can speak without saying everything. Every detail must be precisely stated, every action or position or demonstration explained to the full. This attempt at inclusive precision in statement is defeated by the nature of language (if not by the vestige of narration); *Watt* is the record of that failure. The boundaries of Watt's apprehension are not those of Mr. Knott's household:

Looking at a pot, for example, or thinking of a pot, at one of Mr Knott's pots, of one of Mr Knott's pots, it was in vain that Watt said, Pot, pot. Well, perhaps not quite in vain, but very nearly. For it was not a pot, the more he looked, the more he reflected, the more he felt sure of that, that it was not a pot at all. It resembled a pot, it was almost a pot, but it was not a pot of which one could say, Pot, pot, and be comforted.[2]

That we are logical is no reason everything else must be logical. A sort of burnt offering to the Absurd, *Watt* leaves us with the question: How does a closed system see past itself, and say what it cannot directly say?

Wittgenstein's *Tractatus* is a series of propositions (by definition logical) that by its end has managed to lead us to perceive the mystical, or has shown us where

[2] *Watt*, p. 81.

to start looking. There are no surprises in logic (6.1251); whatever can be put into words can be put clearly. What can be posed as a problem can be answered. But "the solution of the problem of life is seen in the vanishing of the problem" (6.521). For logic, cause-and-effect is a law. We forget that the notion "cause" implies the notion "effect," that "belief in the causal nexus is *superstition*" (5.1361). In reality there must be able to be events that are not caused or causes.[3] Problems and their solutions move in closed systems, but life is not closed; its truths "make themselves manifest" (6.522) and cannot be put into language.

We feel that even when *all possible* scientific questions have been answered, the problems of life remain completely untouched. Of course there are then no questions left, and this itself is the answer. [6.52]

Watt is on the road to answering all possible questions, making all possible statements, on a stack pass in the Library of Babel.

[3] A *first cause*, for example, is demanded by logic to explain the existence of the universe; yet a first cause must have been uncaused, a first cause contradicts the laws of cause and effect, a first cause is outside logic and demands not proof but belief. And if a first cause does not conform to the logical demands concerning causes, how can one within logic predicate a necessary first cause? In a rigorous defense of causality, logic leads straight to religion, but proves the truth neither of causality nor of religion.

Watt and the *Tractatus* generate in the reader an awareness of what is beyond language. The *Tractatus* explains thought and language, shows us that they are closed, that they can deal only with the logical, that every problem they can pose can be answered—then appeals to our sense of what cannot be expressed. We are shown, through language, language's limitations:

Feeling the world as a limited whole—it is this that is mystical. [6.45]

My propositions serve as elucidations in the following way: anyone who understands me eventually recognizes them as nonsensical, when he has used them—as steps—to climb up beyond them. (He must, so to speak, throw away the ladder after he has climbed up it.)

He must transcend these propositions, and then he will see the world aright.

What we cannot speak about we must pass over in silence. [6.54, 7]

The *Tractatus* cannot discuss what cannot be put into language.[4] It does not transcend itself, but points. The reader must use these propositions to transcend them.

[4] Watt, on the other hand, does attempt to discuss what is impossible to discuss—to name, for example, a not-pot. *Watt* makes us aware of the limits of language poetically, through frustrating and exhausting us, while the *Tractatus* simply tells us about these limits. Himself only one of its names, Watt attempts to name the Unnamable.

The *Tractatus* remains logical; it is not poetry or silence. Even poetry, as it is written in language, cannot finally abandon logic, but it can give the illusion of doing so. One of the richest techniques in the generation of this illusion is repetition.

Up to a certain point, repetition emphasizes the sense of what is repeated—builds, as it does in *King Lear*. Beyond that point, the repeated word loses its original meaning: it becomes a routine or cliché, a blank wall, a falsified memory, or a drone. But repeated past this point, the word can become a force, the drone primary sound. By repetition, a proposition can become a secular *mantra*.

The Upanishads attempt to communicate in language an understanding of that reality of which phenomena are the distortion, that Sound of which matter is the lowest frequency. They lead the reader to understanding through repetition and often also through the reduction of language to its suggestive, arational, primary element (the syllable). If all comes from one, then the identity of statements shown through repetition begins the reader's education in reduction (expansion) stylistically. Speech gives the illusion of difference, but it can also lead to an understanding of the fallacy of difference, as it does in this tale from the Chhāndogya Upanishad:

His father said to him: "Svetaketu, as you are so conceited, considering yourself so well-read, and so stern, my dear, have you ever asked for that instruction by which we hear what cannot be heard, by which we know what cannot be known?"

"What is that instruction, Sir?" he asked.

The father replied: "My dear, as by one clod of clay all that is made of clay is known, the difference being only a name, arising from speech, but the truth being that all is clay. . . ." [5]

Svetaketu returns to his father with "all possible scientific questions" answered, and now begins to learn what cannot be taught. The principal tension in the Upanishads is that of language's attempting to transcend itself, to make manifest the nonverbal. Svetaketu is led to see the unity of all things, and the identity of his Self and the life-essence of the universe through his father's repetition:

"Now that which is that subtile essence, in it all that exists has its self. It is the True. It is the Self, and thou, O Svetaketu, art it." [6]

Each time he hears this line, Svetaketu replies, "Please, Sir, inform me still more," and the father agrees, until at the end of the chapter:

[5] Chhāndogya Upanishad, Sixth Prapathaka, in Nicol Macnicol, *Hindu Scriptures* (London: J. M. Dent & Sons, Ltd., Everyman's Library, 1938), p. 166.

[6] *Hindu Scriptures,* pp. 171 ff.

"As that truthful man is not burnt, thus has all that exists its self in That. It is the True. It is the Self, and thou, O Svetaketu, art it." He understood what he said, yea, he understood it. [7]

The father's explanations do not build on each other; each unit of argument makes the same point in a similar way. But after nine units, Svetaketu understands. He does not give in, or "learn," but sees. The communication was not logical but transcendent of logic, through repetition.

The aesthetics of novelty belong to the assumptions of cause and effect. If each pictorial or language unit is seen as leading necessarily to another, and takes its meaning from that relation and progression, it is not possible for each unit to have complete identity; we expect change and development, and see each unit not for what it is but for what it comes from and leads to. We remember and anticipate. But where an event can be an event without being a cause, it can exist on its own and be read or observed for what it is in itself, in its own space and time. Each unit is complete regardless of that to which it looks back or forward. It takes place in the present. It does not lose force in recurring; the repetitious is considered so because it appears to the remembering and anticipating mind that the discussion is not progressing as readily or assuredly as it should,

[7] *Hindu Scriptures,* p. 174.

that it is foundering in the present from a lack of understanding of its larger direction. But units do not necessarily have larger direction; this direction can be something imposed on them from without. Our minds work by logic; they think of things as being causes with effects—but it is certainly possible that they distort what is before them, organize illogical reality to make themselves feel comfortable (as Watt would "be comforted" if his pot could be described "pot"). Mathematics can prove only the truths of mathematics, and logic of logic. Neither system can touch or prove reality, although each may be able to infer it, or occasionally find correspondence with it; falsification is inevitable. It is even possible to say that we reduce the life force we represent to a logically apprehensible "identity," that we make ourselves Mr. B or Miss L as a defense against the immensity of life in and around us. In a Darwinian sense, we are the animal that survived through reason; reason is an accident, and it has always been part of *our* nature, though not necessarily part of that of all phenomena. Our mind arranges experience into cause and effect, perception into logic, time into clock-time, life into personality—defensively, as a way of controlling or defining territory. The concept of personality is a territorial distortion (like arranging one's furniture), making experience easier to deal with; but it is still a distortion. Mathematics, personality, and logic are part of a box or room we have defined for ourselves;

we have closed ourselves in with this box, but we can make the box a step. That is one meaning of the conclusion of the *Tractatus*.

Language attempts to reach indivisibility, the freedom from relegation to "then" or "part" or "name," through repetition. Here is a story from the Brihadaranyaka Upanishad:

The threefold descendants of Prajapati, gods, men, and Asuras [evil spirits], dwelt as Brachmacharins [students] with their father Prajapati. Having finished their studentship the gods said: "Tell us (something), Sir." He told them the syllable da. Then he said: "Did you understand?" They said: "We did understand. You told us 'Damyata,' Be subdued." "Yes," he said, "you have understood."

Then the men said to him: "Tell us something, Sir." He told them the same syllable da. Then he said: "Did you understand?" They said: "We did understand. You told us, 'Datta,' Give." "Yes," he said, "you have understood."

Then the Asuras said to him: "Tell us something, Sir." He told them the same syllable da. Then he said: "Did you understand?" They said: "We did understand. You told us, 'Dayadham,' Be merciful." "Yes," he said, "you have understood."

The divine voice of thunder repeats the same, Da da da, that is, Be subdued, Give, Be merciful. Therefore let that triad be taught, Subduing, Giving, and Mercy.[8]

[8] Brihadaranyaka Upanishad, in Nicol Macnicol, *Hindu Scriptures*, pp. 102–103. "Da" should be left alone rather than talked about, but it might at first be conceptualized as "*Da*　": that

The three differences made by the three audiences out of the one syllable do not falsify the intention of the syllable; "da" is them all. It is the language of nature.

The different names for "clays" create the illusion of difference among clay, but the truth is that all is one—that all selves not simply "have self" but are Self; the repeated syllable "da" is a prelanguage of unity. Repetition makes us see the unity of which names are a distortion, but it must also make us see the fallacy of connections, of *syntax*. We know that there are an infinite number of points in a line, but there are also an infinite number of points in a point. (The Trinity is a similar, equally simple mystery.) The world is and depends on the illusion of difference; realizing that all is one, we are freed from phenomena. Our self returns to, joins, becomes that Self which *is*. We stop drawing lines between the points of our experience, stop saying this is different from and connected to that; we see this *is* that. Names create difference, and syntax creates connections among those differences, allowing them to act on each other in time. But clock-time, of course, is another of these illusions—as the decision to apprehend the present by splitting it into instants forever separates art from the continuity of the real; unity is outside time.

---

is, as containing, unsaid, all of the words that are made out of it. To speak such a word is to speak not only "da," but the simultaneous meanings of the silence it carries: to speak, in effect, the nonverbal as well as the syllable.

(Only in time could there be, as Stein asserts, "a difference between Barcelona.") Syntax allows us to think in terms of petty networks, but it is as faulty and mechanical and unenlightened when considered in relation to Unity (which, having no differences, needs no connections) as the telephone system might be to a group mind. Repetition is minimum syntax: a word relating to and acting on itself. No connection could be less conducive to the consideration of networks, of structures made out of false differences. The word, and then the word. Our mind, taken off "connections," may begin to perceive the One. The word has *all* its reality (within the limits of language) at every use; but the syntax of repetition, undoing those falsifications wrought by the syntax of novelty, takes the word further, into its inherent preverbal timelessness.

Constantine in Berlin

For Kierkegaard, repetition is not only "the whole of life," [9] but in fact, eternity. His *Repetition: An Essay in Experimental Psychology,* published the same day as *Fear and Trembling* (October 16, 1843), is in two parts. The first discusses, in a comic fashion, the possibility

[9] Søren Kierkegaard, *Repetition: An Essay in Experimental Psychology,* trans. Walter Lowrie (Princeton: Princeton University Press, 1941), p. 33; page references are to the 1964 Harper Torchbooks edition.

of repeating actual experience in the phenomenal world. The second, which at its head repeats the title, *Repetition,* abandons "experimental psychology" and deals with repetition in eternity. As Constantine, the comic narrator, defines them:

Repetition and recollection are the same movement, only in opposite directions; for what is recollected has been, is repeated backwards, whereas repetition properly so called is recollected forwards. Therefore repetition, if it is possible, makes a man happy, whereas recollection makes him unhappy—provided he gives himself time to live and does not at once, in the very moment of birth, try to find a pretext for stealing out of life, alleging, for example, that he has forgotten something.[10]

Kierkegaard tells two interrelated stories. The second concerns a young man who falls in love with the idea of a girl he has met; she remains his inspiration as long as they are apart. Recollection inspires his writing, and turns him into a sighing unhappy lover:

His eyes filled with tears, he flung himself down on a chair and repeated the verse again and again. . . . He was in love, deeply and sincerely in love; that was evident, and yet at once, on one of the first days of his engagement, he was capable of recollecting his love. Substantially he was through with the whole relationship. . . . he did not love

[10] *Repetition,* p. 33.

her, he merely longed for her. . . . the love of recollection does indeed make a man unhappy. My young friend did not understand repetition.[11]

The young man is trying to continue his love as if its being over were essential to its attraction; he tries to keep his fiancée distanced (in poetry or melancholy) and remains in a sense unable to enjoy her. But the melancholy drives him too far; the young man renounces his fiancée (as Kierkegaard had his) and the love of recollection; he "remains perfectly still," and in this primal solitude discovers repetition, which he describes as receiving himself back. His emotions had become "falsified" [12] in his affair with the girl; when he gave her up, hoping they might continue in perpetual stasis, she surprised him by marrying someone else. The young man writes to the narrator, Constantine Constantius:

She is married. . . . I am again myself, here I have the repetition, I understand everything, and existence seems to me more beautiful than ever. . . . The discord in my nature is resolved, I am again unified. . . . Is there not a repetition? Did I not get everything doubly restored? Did I not get myself again, precisely in such a way that I must *doubly feel its significance?* And what is a repetition of

[11] *Repetition*, pp. 38, 40, 41.

[12] *Repetition*, p. 41. (Falsified through recollection, or remembering.)

earthly goods which are of no consequence to the spirit—what are they in comparison with such a repetition? Only his children Job did not receive again double, because a human life is not a thing that can be duplicated. In that case only spiritual repetition is possible, although in the temporal life it is never so perfect as in eternity, which is the true repetition. . . . I am born to myself . . . one can hear oneself speak even though the movement goes on in one's own interior—there where one every instant stakes one's life, every instant loses it, and wins it again.[13]

The echo of "beginning again and again" in the final sentence suggests the identity of the great repetition—eternity—and the instants of repetition that are our dynamic life: of the continuous present and the timeless. This spiritual state, of continual repetition (which is one repetition, just as time is a sequence of timeless instants and yet of course not really divisible into instants), is parodied by the first story, which tells of the narrator's attempt to achieve a repetition in action.

[13] *Repetition*, pp. 125–126 [italics mine]. The staking-losing-winning image probably refers to the heartbeat, with each return of life felt more intensely. It is interesting to compare the young man with Stein's St. Therese, who receives herself back from instant to instant of *Four Saints in Three Acts;* for this reason the stage directions insist on her existence even within one of her speeches:

Saint Therese.   Once in a while.
Saint Therese.
Saint Therese.   Once in a while.

Constantine Constantius repeats a trip to Berlin in the hope that he will find the second trip as pleasurable as the first, and to determine whether repetition is possible. He finds that it is not: the rooms where he stayed have been remodeled, the theatre is not as funny, and he himself has changed. Constantine's message is clear:

The young man's problem is, *whether repetition is possible.* It was as a parody of him that I made the journey to Berlin to see whether repetition was possible. The confusion consists in the fact that the most inward problem is here expressed in an outward way, as though repetition, if it were possible, might be found outside the individual, since it is within the individual it must be found, and hence the young man does exactly the opposite, he keeps perfectly still. Accordingly, the consequence of the journey is that I despair of the possibility and then step aside for the young man, who with his religious primitiveness is to discover repetition. . . . The young man transfigures repetition as his own consciousness raised to the second power.[14]

The young man wins himself back not simply from an intense romance but more importantly, from guilt. The eternity he discovers, with its security of individual being and consciousness, is not Stein-secular but religious. And he is free to love "the idea" without writing melancholy poetry to the woman (whom in a sense he

[14] Kierkegaard quoted in Walter Lowrie, "Editor's Introduction," Søren Kierkegaard, *Repetition*, pp. 14–15.

never really knew at all) who was the temporal occasion
of his awakening to that idea. This raising of consciousness to the second power cannot be willed any more
than repetition can be effected in the outer world, or
than voluntary memory can help one repeat a complete
experience. (The Proustian instant is certainly one
where the past is "recollected forwards.") And there is
freedom in this repetition to which "progress" is irrelevant and novelty adolescent. One is oneself, happy,
constant:

Repetition is a beloved wife of whom one never tires. For
it is only of the new one grows tired. Of the old one never
tires. When one possesses that, one is happy, and only he
is thoroughly happy who does not delude himself with the
vain notion that repetition ought to be something new,
for then one becomes tired of it. . . . He who would only
hope is cowardly, he who would only recollect is a volup-
tuary, but he who wills repetition is a man, and the more
expressly he knows how to make his purpose clear, the
deeper he is as a man.[15]

In art, too, repetition is a sign of maturity, of assurance
and strength. The image of the wind in the mountains
is meant to illustrate the way one realizes his personal
possibilities and from them forges a character, but it
makes sense in an aesthetic context as well, where the
artist repeats with assurance—not out of an inability

[15] *Repetition,* pp. 33–34.

to create something new, but as an expression of artistic freedom and intensity:

When in a mountainous region one hears the wind day in and day out execute firmly and unchangingly the same theme, one perhaps is tempted for an instant to ignore the imperfection of the analogy and to rejoice in this symbol of the consistency and assurance of human freedom. One perhaps does not reflect that there was a moment when the wind . . . came to this region as a stranger, flung itself wildly, meaninglessly into the fissures . . . until, after it had learnt to know its instrument, it brought all this into accord in the melody which from day to day it executes unchangeably.[16]

For Kierkegaard, the aesthetics of repetition, the personal will to repetition, and the eternal interest and assurance of repetition in nature are all anticipations of Repetition in eternity. For it is only in a spiritual sense that one is able to discuss true Repetition. Literature takes place in a developing present, and its repetitions must remain near-repetitions. They can only suggest Repetition, just as Eliade's primitive (believing

[16] *Repetition,* p. 59. The last sentences of the young man's last letter to Constantius imitate, with repeating constructions, the repeating ocean waves: the stylistic, natural, and independent tendencies of repetition unified. ("Hail to the breaking wave. . . . Hail to the breaking wave. . . !")

in Repetition) relied on near-repetition of archetypal gestures and actions to place himself in eternity. The literature and religions of the continuous present share the conception of time as a succession of timeless instants, but where primitive man repeated the deeds of other men, Kierkegaard's young man repeats himself, multiplies himself by himself exponentially. Rather than playing a trick on time (starting it over every year, to keep up with it), the lover of Repetition transcends time entirely.

Had Constantine Constantius' trip to Berlin succeeded, it would have been a near-repetition, because it would have occurred in time. Even if he had experienced the same trip, he would have been a different person during the repetition. With himself as his own ancestor, his trip to Berlin demonstrates the fallacy of the Eliadean primitive's attempt at repetition. But it is precisely himself that the young man repeats, always more assuredly, and it is thus that he comprehends eternity.

We discover through repetition that the solution to time is outside of time. The present is always escaping us (time is passing); but on the other hand, we are never in anything but the present. And the continuous present teaches us that "permanence" is a question not of duraion but of intensity and being. If we consider clocks as having the same relation to time as propositions bear to reality, we realize that a clock can tell about time but cannot express or be time. The present is timeless. As Wittgenstein put it:

If we take eternity to mean not infinite temporal duration but timelessness, then eternal life belongs to those who live in the present. [6.4311]

The infinitesimal is infinite; as we live always in the present, we live always:

Death is not an event in life: we do not live to experience death. [6.4311]

The present does not remember the past. By beginning again, our art-time is always present. By repeating a sound until we see past it—whether that sound is a syllable, a religious formula, or our name—we may come not to have to apprehend the present by instants, but may find the continuum of our self in the continuum of the true, and so live in eternity. It is not doing things over that is the key to life in the present, but abandoning the illusions of past and future: attention to that timelessness which is the time of our consciousness and of reality. The sun comes up every day (and we receive it) in perfect attention; it does not fear that it is being repetitious, nor presumably does it remember what it has done before or consider what it will do in the future. It is the strength of assertion, the assurance of identity, that is the force of repetition; it is the apologetic consciousness squeezed between past and future, unsure of itself and its intentions, wavering, faltering, that gives the sense of the repetitious to recurrence. The present is eternal, and eternity is repetition.

Selected Bibliography

(Movies are alphabetized by director.)

Agee, James, and Walker Evans. *Let Us Now Praise Famous Men.* Boston, Houghton Mifflin, 1960.

Beckett, Samuel. *Endgame.* New York, Grove Press, 1958.

——. *Proust and Three Dialogues.* London, John Calder, 1965.

——. *Three Novels* [*Molloy, Malone Dies, The Unnamable*]. New York, Grove Press, 1965.

——. *Waiting for Godot.* New York, Grove Press, 1954.

——. *Watt.* New York, Grove Press, 1959.

Bergman, Ingmar. *Persona.* 1966.

Borges, Jorge Luis. *Labyrinths.* New York, New Directions, 1964.

Brainard, Joe. "Alice," Art and Literature 11. Paris, 1967.

Bridgman, Richard. *Gertrude Stein in Pieces.* New York, Oxford University Press, 1971.

Brown, E. K. *Rhythm in the Novel.* Toronto, University of Toronto Press; London, Oxford University Press, 1950.

Buñuel, Luis. *The Exterminating Angel.* 1962.

Coe, Richard N. *Samuel Beckett.* New York, Grove Press, 1970.

Dieterle, William. *Love Letters.* 1945.

Eisenstein, Sergei M. *Film Form,* trans. Jan Leyda. New York, Harcourt, Brace & World, 1949.

——. *October.* 1927.

——. *Potemkin.* 1925.

Eliade, Mircea. *The Myth of the Eternal Return,* trans. Willard Trask. New York, Pantheon, Bollingen, 1954. [Also available as *Cosmos and History*]

Faulkner, William. *Absalom, Absalom!* New York, Random House, 1936.

——. *Light in August.* New York, Random House, 1932.

Freud, Sigmund. *Beyond the Pleasure Principle,* trans. James Strachey. New York, Liveright, 1924.

——. "Further Recommendations in the Technique of Psycho-Analysis: Recollection, Repetition, and Working Through," *Collected Papers,* Vol. II, trans. Joan Riviere. London, Hogarth Press, 1949.

Genet, Jean. *The Blacks: A Clown Show,* trans. Bernard Frechtman. New York, Grove Press, 1960.

——. *Miracle of the Rose,* trans. Bernard Frechtman. New York, Grove Press, 1967.

Godard, Jean-Luc. *2 ou 3 choses que je sais d'elle.* 1966.

Hemingway, Ernest. *A Farewell to Arms.* New York, Scribner's, 1929.

——. *The Sun Also Rises.* New York, Scribner's, 1926.

Hoffman, Frederick J. *Gertrude Stein.* Minneapolis, University of Minnesota, Pamphlets on American Writers, 1961.

The Holy Scriptures. Philadelphia, Jewish Publication Society of America, 1917.

Hutchins, Robert M. *Zuckerkandl.* Pacifica Radio, 1962. Hubley Studio, 1968.

Kierkegaard, Søren. *Repetition: An Essay in Experimental Psychology,* trans. Walter Lowrie. Princeton, Princeton University Press, 1941.

Kubie, Lawrence S. *Neurotic Distortion of the Creative Process.* New York, Noonday Press, 1961.

LeBorg, Reginald. *The Mummy's Ghost.* 1944.

Léger, Fernand. *Ballet mécanique.* 1924.

Macnicol, Nicol. *Hindu Scriptures.* London: J. M. Dent & Sons, Ltd., Everyman, 1938.

Marcus, Steven. *The Other Victorians.* New York, Basic Books, 1966.

Marker, Chris. *La Jetée.* 1962.

Proust, Marcel. *A la Recherche du temps perdu,* ed. Clarac and Ferré. Paris, NRF, Bibliothèque de la Pléiade, 1963. [Available in English under the title, *Remembrance of Things Past,* trans. Moncrieff and Blossom. New York, Random House.]

Pudovkin, V. I. *Film Technique,* trans. Ivor Montagu, enlarged edition. London, George Newnes, Ltd., 1935.

——. *Mother.* 1926.

Resnais, Alain. *L'Année dernière à Marienbad.* 1961.

——. *Hiroshima mon amour.* 1959.

——. *Je t'aime, je t'aime.* 1968.

——. *Muriel, ou le temps d'un retour.* 1963.

Robbe-Grillet, Alain. *For a New Novel,* trans. Richard Howard. New York, Grove Press, 1965.

——. *Last Year at Marienbad,* trans. Richard Howard. New York, Grove Press, 1962.

——. *Two Novels [Jealousy and In the Labyrinth],* trans. Richard Howard. New York, Grove Press, 1965.

Shakespeare, William. *The Tragedy of King Lear.* c. 1605.

Slatoff, Walter. *Quest for Failure.* Ithaca, Cornell University Press, 1960.

Stein, Gertrude. *Everybody's Autobiography.* New York, Random House, 1937.

——. *Four in America.* New Haven, Yale University Press, 1947.

——. *Last Operas and Plays,* ed. Carl van Vechten. New York & Toronto, Rinehart & Co., Inc., 1949.

——. *Lectures in America.* New York, Random House, 1935.

——. *Portraits and Prayers.* New York, Random House, 1934.

——. *Selected Writings of Gertrude Stein,* ed. Carl van Vechten. New York, Random House, 1962.

Sutherland, Donald. *Gertrude Stein: A Biography of Her Work.* New Haven, Yale University Press, 1951.

Wittgenstein, Ludwig. *Tractatus Logico-Philosophicus,* trans. D. F. Pears and B. F. McGuinness. London, Routledge & K. Paul, 1961.

Yeats, W. B. *Selected Poems and Two Plays of William Butler Yeats,* ed. M. L. Rosenthal. New York, Macmillan, 1966.

Index

Index

Library of Congress Cataloging in Publication Data
(For library cataloging purposes only)

Kawin, Bruce F   , date.
  Telling it again and again.

  Bibliography: p.
  1. Repetition in literature. 2. Repetition in
moving pictures. I. Title.
PN56.R45K3   809.9'2   75-37753
ISBN 0-8014-0698-6